A Gift of Love

Compiled and Edited

by Terri Kalfas

GRACE
PUBLISHING

Scripture references marked CJB are taken from the *Complete Jewish Bible* Copyright © 1998 by David H. Stern. All rights reserved. Used by permission.

Scripture references marked ESV are take from *The Holy Bible, English Standard Version*. ESV® Text Edition: 2016. Copyright © 2001 by Crossway Bibles, a publishing ministry of Good News Publishers. All rights reserved. Used by permission.

Scripture references marked KJV are taken from the *King James Vesion* of the Bible.

Scripture references marked LSB are taken from the *Legacy Standard Bible* Copyright ©2021 by The Lockman Foundation. Managed in partnership with Three Sixteen Publishing Inc. LSBible.org. All rights reserved. Used by permission.

Scripture references marked NASB are taken fom the *New American Standard Bible*, 1995 Copyright © 1960, 1962, 1963, 1968, 1971, 1972, 1973, 1975, 1977, 1995 by The Lockman Foundation, La Habra, CA. All rights reserved. Used by permission.

Scripture references marked NET are taken from *The Net Bible®, New English Translation Bible®* copyright ©1996-2017 by Biblical Studies Press, L.L.C. All rights reserved. Used by permission.

Scripture references marked NIV are taken from *The Holy Bible, New International Version®*, NIV® Copyright ©1973, 1978, 1984, 2011 by Biblica, Inc.® Used by permission. All rights reserved worldwide.

Scripture references marked NKJV are taken from the *New King James Version®*. Copyright © 1982 by Thomas Nelson. Used by permission. All rights reserved.

Scripture references marked NLT are taken from *Holy Bible, New Living Translation*, copyright © 1996, 2004, 2015 by Tyndale House Foundation. Used by permission of Tyndale House Publishers, Inc., Carol Stream, Illinois 60188. All rights reserved. Used by permission.

Royalties for this book are donated to Samaritan's Purse.

A GIFT OF LOVE

ISBN-13: 978-1-60495-101-1

Copyright © 2024 by Grace Publishing House. Published in the U.S.A. by Grace Publishing House. All rights reserved. No part of this book may be reproduced in any form or by any electronic or mechanical means, including information storage and retrieval systems, without permission in writing, except as provided by U.S.A. Copyright law.

From Samaritan's Purse

We so appreciate your donating royalties from the sale of the books in the *Divine Moments* series to Samaritan's Purse.

What a blessing that you would think of us! Thank you for your willingness to bless others and bring glory to God through your literary talents. Grace and peace to you.

Our Mission Statement

Samaritan's Purse, a nondenominational evangelical Christian organization provides spiritual and physical aid to hurting people around the world.

Since 1970, Samaritan's Purse has helped victims of war, poverty, natural disasters, disease, and famine with the purpose of sharing God's love through His Son, Jesus Christ.

Go and do likewise.

Luke 10:37

You can learn more by visiting our website at samaritanspurse.org

Dedicated to the many authors
who have so generously contributed their stories
to the books in the *Divine Moments* series in support of
Samaritan's Purse.

Table of Contents

1. *No Better Gift* ~ Nanette Thorsen-Snipes 7
2. *To Give and Receive* ~ Lin Daniels 8
3. *I Found My Christmas Spirit at the Dollar Store* ~ Phil Gladden 10
4. *The Greatest Gift of Love* ~ Charlene Warren 13
5. *Missing from the Manger* ~ Rachael M. Colby 15
6. *A Not-So-Quiet Christmas* ~ Heather Roberts 17
7. *My Easter Poinsettia* ~ Lauri Lemke Thompson 20
8. *Recapturing the Wonder of Christmas* ~ Cindy W. Arora 23
9. *A Christmas Whirlwind* ~ Nancy Aguilar 26
10. *Taking Time to Give Love* ~ Jeanetta Chrystie 27
11. *The Gift of Harmony* ~ Donna Collins Tinsley 30
12. *The Christmas Barn* ~ Amannda Gail Maphies 33
13. *Follow the Star* ~ Glenda Ferguson 35
14. *Immanuel* ~ Diana Derringer 39
15. *Tidings of Comfort and Joy* ~ Lydia E. Harris 40
16. *All That I Need* ~ Penny L. Hunt 46
17. *Finding Christmas* ~ Barbara Culley 49
18. *Scenes of Life* ~ Helen L. Hoover 57
19. *My Favorite Customs and Moments* ~ Peggy Park 59
20. *A Gift from the Sea* ~ Lola Di Giulio De Maci 62
21. *A Sweet Wonder* ~ Charlene Warren 66
22. *The First Christmas Gift* ~ Majetta Morris 67
23. *Nearness and Belonging* ~ Terry Magness 73
24. *I Have It All This Christmas* ~ Lauri Lemke Thompson 76

25. *The Nativity* ~ Kathy Tharpe 79
26. *A Different Kind of Christmas* ~ Norma C. Mezoe 83
27. *How Joseph Loved Mary* ~ Madonna Pool 87
28. *The Gift* ~ Helen L. Hoover 91
29. *Three Special Gifts* ~ Amannda Gail Maphies 93
30. *Big Red* ~ Sherry Diane Kitts 96
31. *He Became* ~ Bob LaForge 100
32. *The Gift That Hit the Right Note* ~ Ellen Fannon 103
33. *Fragrance of Memories* ~ Iris Long 106
34. *Christmas Without Gifts* ~ Diana Derringer 109
35. *Emmanuel's Song* ~ Jeanetta Chrystie 111
36. *The Legacy of Joe Bell* ~ Beverly Robertson 112
37. *Christmas Redemption* ~ Vicki H. Moss 114
38. *A Country Christmas* ~ Peggy Park 119
39. *Little Drummer Girl* ~ Lauri Lemke Thompson 121
40. *Overflowing* ~ Desiree St. Clair Spears 124
41. *Miracle in a Coat Pocket* ~ Helen L. Hoover 127
42. *The Secret Gift* ~ Gina Stinson 129
43. *Christmas Afterglow* ~ Nancy Aguilar 132
44. *The Gift that Keeps on Giving* ~ Annette G. Teepe 133
45. *O Worship the King* ~ Laura Lee Leathers 137

ABOUT THE AUTHORS 142

1
No Better Gift

Nanette Thorsen Snipes

There is no better gift
Than a baby born of old,
Amidst the cattle lowing,
Among frankincense and gold.

A gift especially wrapped
Not in paper or in bows,
But in Mary's loving arms,
The Child the angels know.

He was wrapped in love eternal;
A Shepherd who gives the call.
He is the wondrous Gift of God,
A Savior for us all.

2

To Give and Receive

Lin Daniels

Our elementary school nurse, Marcia, had a tender, compassionate heart. Especially for young families facing tough times. She kept a confidential list of these folks, and with godly timing would offer them a donated gift card to a local grocery store.

At Thanksgiving, Marcia would post food lists on the inside of her office door. Teachers would bring in vegetables, potatoes, gravy, stuffing, pies, and the like. (And of course, turkeys!) All the fixings needed for a delicious turkey dinner!

Christmas was a particularly difficult time for some families, especially those with young kids. So Marcia organized Christmas baskets — including not only food but also gifts (that a parent had suggested). These presents could be everything from socks, undies, and sweatpants to toys, sporting equipment, and arts and crafts materials. All of these presents were given anonymously — maintaining respect and dignity.

Marcia shared a particularly moving Christmas story with me. A lady had come to her office and asked if she was still doing Christmas baskets. When Marcia replied, "yes," the lady was thrilled and asked if she could contribute to one. Apparently, a few years earlier, this lady's husband had been laid off work right before Christmas. Her family had been the recipient of a Christmas basket that year — and she was extremely grateful! Now, her family was in a better financial position, so she wanted to "sponsor "a Christmas basket — to bless someone, just like she had been blessed!

This story reminds me that sometimes in our lives, we are on the "receiving end" and other times we might be on the "giving end." And God is present in both!

3
I Found My Christmas Spirit at the Dollar Store

Phil Gladden

I struggled to get into the Christmas spirit last year. First, the weather was unseasonably warm, and though I appreciated the good Lord sending us an unexpected overflow of sunbathing weather, it just didn't make sleigh bells ring in my ears or inspire me to sing *Jingle Bells* at the top of my lungs.

Things changed when I went to the nearby dollar store to pick up some whipped cream for my sweet potato pie and I glanced across the street at a church. Outside of the main entrance stood a line of kids in full Nativity attire. I watched young boys dressed in shepherd's robes laughing and jumping excitedly near the sidewalk as they anticipated being the center of attention soon.

On the other side of the sidewalk little girls with angelic faces attempted to fly with wire-framed angel wings. I chuckled when I saw a child who came out dressed as one of the wise men. His bulky costume nearly tripped him until one of the angels — who I felt sure was his older sister — took his hand. Soon, all of the children would march back inside to the delight of parents, grandparents, and all of their church family as they reenacted the coming of Jesus Christ, our Lord and Savior.

I almost abandoned my sweet potato pie to go inside and watch, but my wife, Ruth, was recovering from hip surgery and grew anxious if I stayed away too long.

Hopefully, next year, she'll be fully recovered, and then we'll both go, I thought.

As I strolled into the store, the felt stockings, tinsel, and colorful decorations I saw reminded me of other Christmases. I thought of my Aunt Annette, who took great pride in decorating her Christmas trees. Each year it took her an entire week, and she would forbid anyone from peeking until she completed her task. And each season, she produced a masterpiece that outdid the previous year. She reveled in the compliments and humbly responded to the praise with, "I reckon it'll do, I guess." It was her gift to the family . . . along with hot cider and gingerbread Santa cookies with white-icing beards.

I also recalled the year when I was seven. It was snowing and icicles hung from the power lines like crystal daggers when my father went into Sears to pick up a stand for our tree. There, he noticed two children wearing worn-out hand-me-down shoes that were several sizes too large. They had to shuffle forward to keep the shoes from slipping off of their feet, yet by the way their teeth chattered it was apparent the winter slush had found its way inside anyway. My father took the children next door to J.C. Penney's and bought them both a pair of Buster Browns and two pairs of socks. We gave them a ride home that cold winter night as the wind blew hard and the snow picked back up. My father never sought praise for his generosity, nor was it ever mentioned again. But my brother and I noticed his kind and generous spirit. We were better people for having known him.

It all reminded me of what Christmas is really about. Or at least what it should be.

As I checked out at the dollar store, the young cashier wished me a Merry Christmas. Not in a robotic, retail-motivated tone, but with a beautiful smile, full eye contact, and a sincerity that only comes from the heart.

While on a simple errand for whipped cream, the Christmas spirit found me when it had been nowhere in sight moments earlier. I left the store with a renewed spirit and drove to my warm home and loving wife listening to "Oh Come All Ye Faithful."

Yes, there's always bad going on in the world. It seems it's ready and waiting to rain down on our happiness. But I discovered that having the Christmas spirit isn't so much about finding it. It's more about simply letting it in despite all our earthly challenges.

I hope everyone has the best holiday season ever.

4
The Greatest Gift of Love

Charlene Warren

We have such a limited account of the miraculous nativity event. Film producers and actors attempt to provide something that is sketchy and unrealistic of the virgin birth of our divine Lord and Savior — Jesus Christ. The biblical account also has few details — maybe with reason.

What Mary must have felt about being chosen for this holy honor as she pondered the angel's prophetic message! Did she divinely understand about this magnificent privilege to be able to have a key role in this event that would one day change the world?

It is interesting how Mary had such an open willingness at such a young age to accept the unknown future. Nothing like this had ever taken place before — or after — that amazing moment with the Holy Spirit. It was something unfathomable by the human mind.

We must also consider her betrothed, young Joseph. How could their relationship with one another endure this supernatural and unbelievable event? How was he supposed to believe such an unusual situation when he also encountered a visit from the angel?

One is inclined to wonder what must have been running through Joseph's and Mary's minds at the angel's announcement.

Scripture does not record that it was a regular occurrence in Bible times for a common, youthful girl to be visited by an angelic being. Surely the encounter must have startled her greatly! She would indeed ponder many questions in her mind — how would she tell Joseph of this amazing happening? What would he think? Would he believe the miracle that was about to take place in her? Would his feelings for her change?

There was no way for this young couple to perceive the unique events that were to take place. Who would have thought Mary would deliver a baby in a lowly stable?

And how is it that, at the birth of this infant, she and Joseph would have visitors who were common shepherds from the nearby hillside? Why would shepherds heed the angels' announcement and choose to come to this meager place? Kings were born in royal palaces, weren't they?

And what about the Magi traveling from afar? They would bring gifts of gold, frankincense, and myrrh. Majestic gifts for a common babe. Surely this couldn't be!

Why too, would Mary, Joseph, and the babe need to flee from King Herod? Why would the king be fearful of such a tiny innocent child as this?

This magnificent story would be left incomplete were it not realized the significance of a word that must be considered here: the Faith . . . and Trust of our main characters, Mary and Joseph, in God Almighty.

They had little awareness that their own lives had been marked from birth, or of the significance of the destiny God had on their lives with the birth of this precious little gift from above.

5
Missing from the Manger

Rachael M. Colby

In the year of our meager manger scene, a snowman made of sand, a lone shepherd, and two sheep showed up for the annual frenzied day-of-decoration at our home . . . sans Mary, Joseph, Jesus, or anyone else.

However, I was glad to see that the "Holy Ghost" adorned his usual spot where an angel would normally rest on other people's nativity scenes. Ariel, our oldest child, was five years old when she presented this treasure made with frayed, pink fabric, a cotton ball, and triangular paper wings to us at Christmas. She declared he was an angel, but my husband and I thought he looked more like a ghost and decided he must represent the Holy Ghost. Ever since his arrival, we've placed him atop our manger scene. His wing bears Ariel's bold signature — as well as Abby's, our youngest daughter. Jealous over the attention Ariel garnered for her ragged rendition, Abby added her name.

"Where is the rest of the nativity set?" I asked our son.

Andrew shrugged and lumbered away. "I have no idea. I looked everywhere."

"Suuure you did."

The manger crew had been all together when I unwittingly

set up their demise and allowed Abby and Andrew to put the ornaments away the year before. Or perhaps that's what happens when you send a teen boy into the attic to bring down the Christmas stuff.

With no time to hunt or shop for a new manger scene, I stuck the Christmas floral arrangement from our neighbor in front of it. Maybe no one would notice that Jesus was missing.

Not exactly a picture-perfect Hallmark-home-for-the-holidays.

But then the real Holy Spirit whispered, "It doesn't matter if Jesus is missing from your manger as long as He resides within your heart."

How true and grand this gentle reminder, to place my hope in Jesus, my redeemer, and put my trust in Him! God stepped down from heaven took the form of a baby and lay in a manger. Holy God incarnate humbled, Immanuel wrapped in human skin. He lived, He died, and rose to save, offering forgiveness for my sin.

How futile my attempts to hide my brokenness, my lonely, hollow heart, with busyness and pretty things, and shallow worldly accolades! Jesus sees, loves, and calls me to come just as I am.

There's no need to hide my flaws and failures, for He turns broken into beautiful when I give myself to Him. Out of chaos, He brings order, lights the way to walk through this dark and weary world. He fills my deepest longings and satisfies from within. Monetary gain and glitz and glamor pale against this blessed hope and healing, and His love that never fails.

Jesus — Gift of gifts given to us, and grace to live for Him. Will you open your heart today and invite the Lord Jesus in?

6
A Not-So-Quiet Christmas

Heather Roberts

This chaotic, but full, Christmas story begins on a cold November night, complete with icy rain and treacherous roads. Our twin sons were due January 9, but that didn't stop my water from breaking just after midnight on November 12. As my astonished husband bumped the hospital bag down our front steps, he repeatedly mumbled, "But it's not time yet." He raced our van, slipping and swerving on icy roads, to the hospital.

The medical team scheduled an emergency C-section for the following morning.

Born eight weeks early, the twins defied all odds. At their birth, we were told that they wouldn't leave until their original due date at the earliest. Yet one child went home with us within four weeks, and the other at four weeks and three days. They earned their early graduation from the Neonatal Intensive Care Unit by achieving the milestones of weighing four pounds and consistently being able to breastfeed.

We arrived home a mere two weeks before Christmas, enduring another storm as we clutched carriers, with newborns tucked into them, while dodging pelting slush between the van and our front door.

We were home, but now what?

Breastfeeding twins was the most difficult and most rewarding job I've ever had. The boys nursed every hour, but not always at the same time and they sometimes took thirty minutes to complete a feeding. I was running on only one hour of consecutive sleep a night. My weight plummeted to thirty pounds below my pre-pregnancy weight. Bruises covered my body due to my extreme underweight status. No matter how much I ate I could not seem to eat enough. My church life group kept us alive by delivering food to the house every other day.

No Christmas tree or any decorations adorned our house that year. Thankfully we had a touch of festivity because a beloved co-worker blessed the boys with Christmas onesies complete with little hats and knit Christmas stockings with their names on them. My mother-in-law visited and helped take pictures of our new little family with the boys in their adorable outfits. Their tiny elf hats looked enormous on their perfect little heads, full of hair despite their premature status. My husband and I held them, perched on pillows between us, their little bodies snuggled into that precious newborn curl.

Three days before Christmas the sudden realization hit that I had purchased no Christmas presents for my husband — or anyone else, for that matter. Scratching my head, I resigned myself to the fact that this Christmas would go on without gifts.

Somehow my sleep-deprived brain recalled that at a baby shower we had received First Christmas ornaments for the boys.

On Christmas Eve, we heated a church-delivered Christmas dinner of meatloaf in the microwave. Then we snuggled into our queen-sized bed, which seemed to shrink daily as baskets of diapers and ointments lined the foot board and end tables.

I handed the two ornaments, jammed into a simple Christmas sack, to my husband.

"How in the world did you have time for this?" He whispered to avoid waking the twins bundled in the bassinets within inches of our bed.

"The same way we've managed this ongoing miracle — with a lot of help from our friends and family, and the good Lord providing for our every need."

God supplied the real gift that year with the survival and later thriving of our twins, as well as the strengthening of our marriage, and the revelation of His gift to us of selfless friends and family members. That year, Christmas certainly didn't hold many sparkling decorations and presents, but in those quiet moments of lucid wakefulness, we held each other tight, content that we were going to make it.

7
My Easter Poinsettia

Lauri Lemke Thompson

I bought a two-dollar poinsettia plant at Walmart the day after Christmas. The first day of spring passed, and the bright red plant was still blooming its little heart out. Outdoors, daffodils and tulips had already peaked, and redbuds and dogwoods were all abloom. Stores were filled with Easter baskets, bunnies and bonnets. Well, okay, maybe not bonnets.

The plant said "never mind" to all this spring hoopla, insisting on touting Christmas. Tiny new reddish-green leaves appeared often — leaves that gradually turned to brilliant scarlet as they grew. In fact, spring brought on quite a growth spurt.

I followed no elaborate instructions to keep this thing alive. I did nothing except set it on a sunny counter and douse it with water every four or five days . . . if I remembered. It seemed whenever I threw away a dead leaf, the plant hurried to replace it with two more.

Thriving, this living symbol of Christmas showed no respect for our calendar. It did not recognize that it had been nearly three months since the Christmas spirit of we humans had wilted away, and that we were heading full throttle toward spring fever, even dreaming of summer days.

In March, almost daily I thought, "I really should throw that thing in the trash. It looks silly." But because I love all things botanical that demonstrate a love for life, except weeds, it stayed in my kitchen.

Perhaps my stubborn poinsettia was meant to be a reminder.

As we made our Easter breakfast reservations, I pondered that the glory we anticipate on Easter did not happen without the pain of Lent. And Lent was preceded by Christmas — Christmas, which is joyful and celebratory like Easter, but which carries with it a message of sacrifice. Our Savior left a perfect Heaven for a dirty stable. The cross shadowed His cradle before the sun shone on His empty tomb. Christmas, Lent, and Easter are all part of God's redemptive plan for humankind.

I finally determined what to do about my poinsettia that year: I would do all I could to keep it alive until Easter. Maybe I would even treat it to a dose of plant food. And then, on that very special Sunday, I would trash it. But only after I took a moment to contemplate that those scarlet leaf points represent drops of blood my Savior shed for me. I would pause to remember the scourges, the thorns, the nails and the sword — for they all drew blood. One could say that blood drops were sown in soil that produced Easter lilies.

I would set my new Easter lily plant on the kitchen counter beside the brave Christmas plant. I would gaze at both plants: the vivid crimson beside the pure white. And I would be grateful for how the two combine to tell the whole amazing story . . . a true story, and one that offers us victory and eternal life. Then, before serving the Easter ham — and to avoid being called a crazy lady — I would put that that spunky poinsettia into the garbage can at last, it having served its purpose extremely well.

And that's exactly what I did.

I pray for you, my reader, to fully understand what His birth, death, and resurrection mean — and to fully experience the great love He has for you.

8
Recapturing the Wonder of Christmas
A Short Story

Cindy W. Arora

Assuredly, I say to you, unless you are converted and become as little children, you will by no means enter the kingdom of heaven. Therefore whoever humbles himself as this little child is the greatest in the kingdom of heaven.

Matthew 18:3-4 NKJV

"Look, Mommy, it's snowing!" my toddler squealed. I stopped my work to take my wide-eyed daughter outside.

I smiled as I watched Sarah trying to catch the large fluffy snowflakes floating down. We admired the fragile design of each snowflake before it melted.

"God made each snowflake," I told her. "No two are alike."

As she continued catching snowflakes, I caught her wonder. I marveled at the sheer volume of individual and intricate snowflakes that have fallen since the beginning of time. How many quadrillion snowflakes has God created?

Before I heard her delighted squeal, I had been struggling

to find joy. I felt exhausted from holiday activities. My busyness had squelched any joy I might feel. How could I recapture the wonder of Christmas?

My breathless holiday pace had eliminated time to pause and reflect on the miraculous around me. I wanted the breathlessness of my life reserved for His wonder. Sarah seemed to live in a perpetual state of wonder. That humbled me. How could I humble my heart before God?

Pausing to reflect on the miracle of snowflakes melted my heart. I resolved to see even what seems mundane with an artist's eye. In that light, the distant mountains became diamonds sparkling in the sunshine. My Sarah's giggle sounded like tinkling bells.

My spiritual discipline of Bible reading, worship, and prayer also opened my heart to His wonder. I resolved to start to tune into the spiritual realities around me and let God surprise me with His wonder every day.

I scooped up Sarah and headed for the kitchen. As she enjoyed her hot cocoa, I read the story of Jesus's birth from Luke 2 aloud.

I considered how, like snowflakes, God uniquely designs and fashions each newborn baby. How, of the eight billion people on the planet, and all the billions who came before, no two are exactly alike.

I reflected on how baby Jesus was not only unique in His humanness, He was also the only God-man. Jesus was fully human and yet He is fully God. Jesus laid aside His godly powers and royal crown to become a helpless baby. The Creator of all became the created.

The sacred beauty of baby Jesus was the Sunrise; God's

tender mercy birthing the dawn of a new era. He is the Light of the world Who shines upon those who sit in darkness and the shadow of death (Matthew 4:16). His light will guide our feet onto the pathway of peace (Luke 2:78-79).

Finally, the Prince of Peace possessed my heart. I inhaled peace. Sarah finished her cocoa and ran off to explore her next wonder. I lingered in God's presence. As I focused on His beauty and His glory, joy bubbled up from within me. I recaptured the wonder of Christmas anew.

9
A Christmas Whirlwind

Nancy Aguilar

Christmas is like a whirlwind,
Spinning me round and round.
Faster and faster I twirl,
As shopping,
Wrapping,
And decorating
Swoosh past,
Leaving me in a heap,
Overwhelmed and weary.

Lord, please pull me out of the whirlwind,
And lead me to that quiet stable,
Where shepherds knelt before You.
Let me linger in the stillness
Of the Baby with His mother,
Until all I see at Christmas
Is Your birth,
Your love,
Your peace.

10

Taking Time to Give Love

Jeanetta Chrystie

My grandmothers showed me it's important to enjoy our loved ones while we have them and take frequent pleasure in doing something special for them. One grandmother made my favorite peach cobbler every Christmas. The other gave me tubs of her homemade persimmon butter, my favorite jam.

After each of my grandfathers graduated to Heaven, I began writing each grandmother on weekends. I wrote about whatever was happening in my life. My maternal grandmother said, "Thank you for the letters and lovely postcards! I've never traveled far and enjoy the pictures, especially the lovely gardens." My paternal grandmother hugged me often, saying, "I love reading your newsy letters, they make me happy every time one is in the mail." Both grandmothers expressed such joy about receiving my letters, that I continued writing them for over twenty years. I enjoyed knowing I was blessing my sweet grandmothers with attention. And every Christmas I was rewarded with "Thank you" and my favorite edible treats.

Some of my letters were long and belabored not only what I was doing but also how I felt about it. Some were short and read more like a list of activities and appointments. Others were postcards of places I was visiting on a vacation or business trip. Each grandmother continued to tell me how much she enjoyed receiving my letters and postcards. They also enjoyed being able to read them over and over whenever they felt lonely or disconnected.

Taking the time to show love is one way to treasure our relationships, at Christmastime and throughout the year.

I extended my letter-writing habit to include a young nephew who was learning to read, my widowed mother-in-law, and several missionaries. Taking time to write personal letters won't result in worldwide fame. It simply blesses people I love who I know enjoy and need contact. It also allows the Holy Spirit to continue to develop in me a more thoughtful and caring spirit for others.

During one cold December visit to my parents' home for Christmas, my mother asked me to take her to visit her mother in a care center, and then to her mother's recently unoccupied house to search for treasured items. On a shelf in my grandmother's closet were shoe boxes stuffed with my letters and postcards! Reduced to tears, I stopped to finger through a few and read about my past life. I wondered what insights my unintentional journal of letters and cards would provide into my spiritual growth over those years and determined to read each of them in the coming months.

When I also gathered a bookshelf full of my grandmother's collection of poetry books, I found several of my lengthier letters on which she had written little notes and prayers. I felt stunned. She had prayed over many of my letters, for me.

Her unexpected Christmas gift to me that year was

invaluable. I thought I was the one giving little gifts of love, but one godly grandmother had faithfully showered me with loving prayers over the years. While I didn't have the opportunity to search for keepsakes my other grandmother may have saved, I feel certain she also offered many prayers on my behalf. By taking the time to share my life and feelings, especially when I was going through difficult times — including a battle with cancer at age twenty-one, I was being upheld in prayers. Even though my grandmothers didn't often try to write back, I knew they highly valued feeling more involved in their eldest grandchild's life.

Today I treasure owning my maternal grandmother's Bible with all of her margin notes and dates, a more recent and precious Christmas gift to me.

It's easy to think of gifts as only physical things. Taking time to know someone well enough to choose meaningful physical gifts is great. But perhaps the real gift is the thought and time we put into our relationships, loving others in the ways they need it most. When we give such gifts, they can return to us in blessings we cannot imagine.

11

The Gift of Harmony

Donna Collins Tinsley

If possible, so far as it depends on you, live peaceably with all.

Romans 12:18 ESV

I once saw a video clip of three people impromptu singing in their kitchen. Their beautiful harmony impressed me.

They looked like two brothers and a sister. She made me think of myself, because it was obvious she was dressed to stay warm in her stay-at-home clothes and big house-shoes. They may have looked a bit like a motley crew, as we are in so many of my favorite family pictures, but the harmony between them and in the melody, was so very beautiful.

I remember days like that. Having a song in my heart and nothing was going to stop it from coming out. There may have even been a dance to go along with it. I felt like I was dancing on a stage for my Lord. It may not even have been during a happy time in my life. If that was the case, then my song and dance were a sacrifice of praise to the Lord. I hope it pleased Him.

This trio's song also made me think about harmony in relationships and what a gift that is. There's the harmony of first love, when you want to be together all the time. Then comes the harmony of love that is a symphony on your wedding day. There's the harmony of a good parent-child relationship. The harmony of a certain kind of friendship, where you do things together, talk often and know that you can tell this person anything and their love will cover you.

Dictionaries tell us harmony is agreement, accord, harmonious relations, or the simultaneous combination of tones blended into chords pleasing to the ear.

However, in thinking about harmony, I can't overlook the fact that some people are in discord. It can be a father or mother's, husband or wife's nightmare. Sometimes it doesn't take much to send things on a downward spiral in families. How do we get and keep harmony in our homes and lives? It really takes more than just one person to resolve discord. But one thing life has taught me is that what one person says or does can contribute to peace or chaos. It takes a daily prayer to be the best person we can be, so we can see the best in others.

The older I get the more I want to be in harmonious relationships, those that bring peace to our souls.

Really, for the most part, each of us is just doing the best we can with what we have. Sometimes, even though we are trying, we haven't quite arrived in that state of mind that thinks good things and does good things for others. It just might not be God's timing for us. If you are struggling with harmony in relationships, go back and pray, search the scriptures, find some music, do something good for someone else.

This Christmas, my wish is for you to be able to live in perfect love and harmony, full of peace, serenity, and gratitude. And I hope you hear a song full of the most beautiful harmony about the real reason for the season. His name is Jesus.

Harmonize Your To-Do List

- Buy presents or be present with the one you are with, giving them full attention.
- Wrap gifts or wrap someone in a hug, a real, deep, heartfelt one.
- Send gifts or send love that lets the recipient know you will never give up on them.
- Shop for food or donate food or acts of kindness and service.
- Make cookies or make memories of times together doing something, even walking.
- See the lights or be the light as you reflect the true light of the world.

12

The Christmas Barn

Amannda Gail Maphies

On my way home from battling last-minute Christmas shoppers and errand runners (stubborn procrastinators much like myself), I turned upon the familiar highway leading to my house. Amongst the swiftly moving traffic, I found myself wishing I had magical powers to automatically transport myself from one location to another, without driving. Not only was I in desperate need of a bathroom, but I had just spent the past two hours among the hordes of shoppers at the local mall. I needed to be free of people, traffic, bustling, stop signs, and all things commercialized in disguise as *merry*. I was in full-on bah-humbug mode, wishing my way home where my furry critters, comfy loungewear, and a welcome glass of my favorite beverage awaited me.

When what to my wondering eyes should appear. . . .

No, not eight tiny reindeer, but rather an old red barn, standing in the midst of a familiar field. I drive this route every single day, yet never had I noticed this dilapidated old wooden barn. Perhaps it blends in with the tall grass and brush inhabiting the empty field surrounding the old structure.

The barn stood out to me on this day, because it hosted a very simple outline, its shining white lights brightly illuminating a Christmas tree on the side of the barn. It was a precious sight. So simple, yet so beautiful. It reminded me of how I envision the timeless nativity. Simple, yet elegant. Rustic, yet refined. Dilapidated, yet somehow worthy of a second glance. And a third.

I could not help but slow down and stare at the meager but festive sight in the otherwise empty field I daily take for granted.

The scene of the original nativity was simple. It was a barn. With dirty, smelly, likely hungry animals. A manger full of soggy old hay. Yet, it housed a tiny king. The Savior of the world. The Messiah that was, is, and is to come.

When we take a moment to pause in this fast-paced rush of holiday mayhem, we can find the true magic of Christmas. Rugged, dirty, unassuming, yet filled with promise, majesty, and a miraculous, true story that will be told for countless future generations, it offers a source of hope in an often dark and hopeless world.

Could it be that the most meaningful gifts we receive this year are those wrapped in packages not traditionally shiny, beautiful, eye-catching, and glorious? Gifts such as gratitude, prayerful consideration, empathy for our fellow man, and a tender heart open to the needs of others? As in the simple, shining outline of a Christmas tree against the starkly rugged old barn, may you find joy in unexpected places at the busy, hustling and bustling, and at times, force-fed magical time of year.

May the simple promise realized with the birth of a precious baby boy hundreds of years ago fill your soul with a tiny light that continues to grow until it becomes a fiery, raging explosion which propels you toward a brand-new year.

13
Follow the Star

Glenda Ferguson

The temperature was in the lower 30s and snow covered the Indiana ground. I jerked one more sweatshirt over my other layers of clothing. My attitude was just as chilly as the early December evening.

This was my first year as an actor in our church's outdoor Christmas drama "Follow the Star." It also just happened to be the first time snow had fallen in our three-year history. In the past I had helped with publicity, a warm and cozy indoor job. But this year, when two senior church members couldn't volunteer outdoors any longer, I agreed to take their place in the village of Bethlehem for two nights. Now I was regretting my decision.

"I can't believe we're going ahead with the program," I said to my husband, Tim.

"Everyone is looking forward to it. It's how they start their Christmas season," he replied as he dressed in his bejeweled wise man costume, then glued on his fake beard.

Recreating the scenes on the night Jesus was born required most of our church family, and other volunteers from our community. We had been planning for an entire year by sewing costumes, scheduling visitors, and giving away tickets.

I know it sounds like such a cliché, but in this case it really did take a village.

So I slipped my colorful striped tunic over my layers of clothing and tied my rope belt. The hem touched the ground, hiding my insulated boots. I covered my head with a matching striped cloth that concealed my knitted hat.

When we pulled up to the church, parking-lot volunteers were clearing the snow. Inside, volunteers grouped our visitors into family units of fifteen. Two guides, often a husband and wife team, walked the families along the trail through the village by following the star.

I followed Tim up the hill behind the church. At the seven-foot wooden gate, one of the Roman soldiers yelled, "Halt!" That was our youth pastor towering over us. Some of the guards were mounted on horses.

We continued up the cleared trail where Tim and the other Magi met the groups around the campfire. Two camels rested inside a wire pen.

"I can't wait to see the kids' reactions," Tim said. "I'll tell them the third camel is on vacation."

The fire felt so good I wanted to stay. But I walked by myself up the wooded trail lit by tiki torches. The local 4-H members, dressed in their shepherd costumes, herded sheep and lambs. Farther ahead, the angels practiced a traditional hymn. Our six-foot-five-inch pastor was filling in for an absent angel. With the spotlight shining on the high stage and him on it, I finally understood the meaning of the words "Fear not" spoken whenever the heavenly beings appeared in the Bible.

Closer to the village, I heard the musicians tuning up their stringed instruments. Volunteer carpenters had constructed Bethlehem with seven wooden shops. Each "merchant" prepared samples of their wares, such as cloth for the children, as well as soup, bread, cheese, roasted meat, and spices. The visitors' tour would end at the inn and the stable just beyond the village.

When I arrived at my shop, I plugged in the small hot plate to warm up honey, then filled wooden bowls with crackers. One of the church members placed a heater right by my frozen feet.

We gathered for a prayer before the visitors arrived.

As many as thirty people visited in the village every forty minutes. I interacted with each group and offered them honey and crackers. After three hours, the last scheduled group arrived. My shoulders drooped, and I managed a couple more greetings.

A guide named Bill must have noticed I was getting tired. "Why don't you come with my group now so you can see how we end the tour?" he suggested.

I quickly tidied up my shop then blended in with the others.

As we approached the inn, Bill quieted everyone down, then said, "Family, we are very tired after our long journey and need a safe place to spend the night." He chose two of the children to knock on the door.

The innkeeper asked what they wanted and replied, "There is no room!"

As I looked at the children's innocent eyes and heard their pleading, I wondered how anyone could have turned them down. We were directed to the stable area filled with loose straw and bales of hay, a donkey and sheep, and Mary and Joseph. The evening was much too cold for a real baby, so a life-like doll lay in the manger. After all the hustle of the evening, the peaceful scene calmed me and the rest of the group. Even the children stood still.

Bill led us in singing "Silent Night."

I glanced up at our brightly lit star. The large wooden shape had been constructed by one of our church family and hung high in the tree. It was shining right over my shop.

During all this busy time, I had forgotten to look up at the star. Now I was filled with a wonderful warm feeling, and realized I actually hadn't noticed the cold for quite some time.

Even though I experienced the hard work, hectic schedule, and time commitments to our program, I still thought the entire evening was filled with all the wonder, hope, and peace of the Christmas season. I couldn't wait to be there with my church family a second night.

14

Immanuel

Diana Derringer

God's presence came to us,
ready to guide us,
seeking to enter our lives.
God has a plan for us
far better than our plans.
God's will or ours?
We must choose.
Will we allow God to live in us,
work through us, transform us?
We gain everything if we give God our all.

"Look! The virgin will conceive a child! She will give birth to a son, and they will call him Immanuel, which means 'God is with us.'"

Matthew 1:23 NLT

15
Tidings of Comfort and Joy

Lydia E. Harris

'Tis the season for "tidings of comfort and joy" found in Christmas carols, greeting cards, and food!

The holidays evoke many comforting memories for me, and some include food. During my childhood, one of the food traditions our family enjoyed was my mother's fruitcake. I know, fruitcake often gets a bad rap. But in our large family with eight children, we all loved it. That might have been the problem.

Mother baked fruitcake around Thanksgiving and let it age until Christmas. But one Christmas, when she went to the pantry to get the fruitcake, she found a knife and a partially eaten cake. Unknown to any of us, each morning on his way to work my brother had been cutting a slice to take for his lunch. We didn't hold it against him. Instead, we laughed that he got away with his caper. After all, it was the season of "good will toward men."

This year for the holidays, how about bringing comfort and joy by hosting a Christmas tea using familiar foods made with a festive twist. This trio of comfort foods is sure to bring glad tidings. Recipes are included.

1. Holiday Scones: ("Visions of sugarplums danced in their heads.")

Use a favorite scone recipe or box mix and add festive ingredients. For example, add 1 cup of candied cherry pineapple mix to the recipe. Or replace candied fruit with red and green gumdrops snipped into small pieces. Or add dried cranberries and white chocolate chips. Cut the scones into Christmas shapes such as stars and bells.

After baking, drizzle the warm scones with a powdered sugar glaze. Decorate the scones with candied cherries, small pieces of gumdrops, or sprinkles.

2. Christmas Tree Sandwiches: ("O Christmas Tree")

Using a tree-shaped cookie cutter and a few extra ingredients, a cucumber-and-cream-cheese sandwich becomes festive. How lovely (and tasty) are your branches!

Cut bread slices and cheddar cheese slices into tree shapes with a cookie cutter. Spread the bread (trees) with cream cheese and top with cheddar-cheese trees. Use a fork to score the peel of a cucumber, then cut it into thin slices. Place half slices of cucumber on the cheese layer in a shingled fashion with scored peeling edges facing down. Add tiny pieces of red pepper or pomegranate seeds as ornaments. Top with a small cheese star.

3. Sweets and JOY! (Joy to the World!)

I met Joy more than forty years ago on a flight. We've kept in touch as pen pals ever since. She sent me her cheesecake recipe, which she used in her sixth-grade home economics class. I made a few changes to the recipe and called it Merry Cherry Cheesecake.

Use your favorite cheesecake recipe or buy a ready-made refrigerated or frozen one. Then top the cheesecake with a can of cherry pie filling. Or turn it into a Merry Berry Cheesecake by serving it with strawberries or raspberries. Sweets add a grand finale to any teatime or meal.

Brew a holiday blend of tea and enjoy past Christmas traditions or create new ones. With these recipes or your favorites, you can remember that "Silent Night" long ago and turn your holidays into a season of "comfort and joy."

From Lydia's Recipe File

Holiday Scones

Ingredients
- 2 C. flour
- ¼ C. granulated sugar
- 1 Tbsp. baking powder
- ½ tsp. salt
- 1¼ C. whipping cream, unwhipped
- ½ tsp. vanilla
- 1 C. (8 oz.) candied cherry pineapple mix, divided

Glaze
- 1 C. powdered sugar
- 1 tsp. butter, softened
- 2 to 3 tsp. milk
- ¼ tsp. vanilla

Directions
1. Preheat the oven to 400 degrees. Lightly grease a baking sheet with nonstick cooking spray.
2. In a bowl, mix together flour, sugar, baking powder, and salt.
3. Cut 5 red and 5 green candied cherries in half and save them to garnish the baked scones.
4. Cut remaining candied fruit pieces into fourths and stir them into the flour mixture to coat them.
5. Add whipping cream and vanilla, and mix.
6. On a lightly-floured surface, knead the dough gently until combined. If it is too dry, add another tablespoon of cream.
7. Roll the dough ½ inch thick. Cut the dough into circles, wedges, or squares.
8. Bake the scones for 12 to 15 minutes, or until lightly browned.
9. While the scones bake, mix the glaze ingredients together.
10. Remove the scones from the oven and place them on a cooling rack. Cool slightly.
11. Dip fork tines into the glaze and drizzle it across the scones. Decorate with half a cherry on top of each.
12. Serve the scones warm with jam, honey, butter, or whipped cream.

Makes about 16 scones.

Variations: Replace candied fruit with red and green gumdrops snipped into small pieces. Or use dried cranberries and white chocolate chips.

Christmas Tree Sandwiches

Ingredients
- Slices of wheat bread (or your favorite kind)
- Thin slices of cheddar cheese
- Cream cheese spread (plain or herb flavored)
- English cucumber
- Red pepper (or pomegranate seeds)
- 4-inch Christmas tree cookie cutter
- ½-inch star-shaped cutter
- Salt and pepper, optional

Directions
1. Cut bread slices into tree shapes with cookie cutter (2 per slice). Plan on 2 or 3 trees per person.
2. Cut cheddar cheese slices into tree shapes with a cookie cutter. Using cheese scraps, cut small stars for the top of the trees.
3. Lightly spread the bread (trees) with cream cheese. Top each with a cheddar-cheese tree.
4. Use a fork to score the peel of the cucumber. Cut cucumber into thin slices.
5. Cut the slices into halves. Place cucumber pieces on top of the cheese layer in a shingled fashion with scored-peel edges facing down. Trim pieces to fit as needed.
6. Cut red pepper into tiny pieces and add a few on top of the cucumber branches for ornaments. Add a cheese star on top.
7. Serve immediately or refrigerate sandwiches in a covered container until ready to serve. Pass salt and pepper with the sandwiches.

Merry Cherry Cheesecake

Ingredients

Crust
20 graham crackers, crushed
½ C. butter, melted

Filling
1 (8-oz.) package cream cheese softened
½ C. granulated sugar
1 egg, beaten
2 tsp. lemon juice
1 tsp. lemon zest
1 tsp. vanilla extract

Topping
1 C. sour cream
2 Tbsp. sugar
½ tsp. vanilla
1 (21 oz.) can cherry pie filling

Directions
1. Preheat oven to 300 degrees.
2. Place the graham crackers into a zip-loc plastic bag and crush them with a rolling pin.
3. Mix crushed crackers and melted butter; press into a 9-inch pie pan (bottom and sides) to make a crust.
4. Combine all filling ingredients in a medium-sized bowl. Beat thoroughly.
5. Pour filling into pie shell. Bake for 30 minutes. Cool.
6. For topping, combine sour cream, sugar, and vanilla. Spread on top of chilled cheesecake. Chill overnight.
7. Top with cherry pie filling. Or cut and serve individual pieces of cheesecake and top each piece with a spoonful of cherry pie filling.

Serves 6 to 8.
Variation: Serve with strawberries or raspberries for a Merry Berry Cheesecake.

16

All That I Need

Penny L. Hunt

The biggest box under the tree stood out like a beacon, tagged with a tantalizing "To Penny from Santa." Though the festive wrapping paper matched the other gifts and was a dead giveaway to our sharp-eyed kids now savvy enough to know the true identity of Santa, they gleefully played along, their eyes sparkling with curiosity and anticipation.

The morning's designated Gift Elf eagerly hefted the giant box and placed it in front of me with a dramatic flourish. Wonder replaced joy as I peeled back the wrapping paper to reveal the surprise inside.

I clasped my hands to my chest, let out an ecstatic "Ohhhh," raised them to my cheeks and giggled. "It's a one-cup-at-a-time coffee maker! Just what I've been dreaming of for so long!"

Santa hinted with a playful wink, "Is that all there is? You better look underneath the coffee maker."

Curious, I set aside the coffee maker box and discovered another below it tied with a red satin ribbon. With eager anticipation, I untied the ribbon and opened the lid. Nestled inside was an array of coffee pods surrounding another box tied with a white satin ribbon. This box held a stunning floral mug made of fine English china. Inside the mug was a card that read, "Better Together," along with a gift certificate for a dozen donuts from my favorite donut shop.

With a hug to my husband, I headed for the kitchen, saying, "I'll be right back. Don't open another gift until I get here. Santa brought me everything I needed for a perfect cup of coffee, and I'm going to make one right now!"

"Good idea," said my husband. "I want some eggnog." And we all headed to the kitchen for early-morning Christmas treats.

"Wow!" exclaimed our youngest, still wearing her candy cane footie pajamas, her eyes wide with wonder. "Look at that!"

On the plate we'd left for Santa and his reindeer were bits of carrot, scattered cookie sprinkles, and beside it, an empty glass of milk. With a delighted grin, she licked a finger, stuck a sprinkle to it, and popped it into her mouth. "Santa really loved our cookies!" she said, her face beaming.

Holding up the remnants of a half-eaten carrot like a trophy, she continued, "And the reindeer enjoyed their treat too!" Her excitement was contagious as she danced around the kitchen, full of holiday joy.

"Well, no wonder Santa's so fat," chimed in the oldest of the bunch. "Imagine how many cookies and goodies he has to eat on Christmas eve just to be polite."

"Santa didn't eat our cookies just to be polite," insisted one of our sweet cookie makers. "He liked our cookies and the milk too. And the reindeer liked the carrots. They just didn't have enough time to eat them all. Imagine how thirsty and hungry they must get flying all around the world!"

"Whatever." The all-knowing older sibling, rolled his eyes.

"How's that coffee coming?" asked my husband. "Let me help you fill the water canister."

Together we had the machine up and working in no time. Watching the first brew warm and fill my beautiful new mug, I smiled, thinking of what fun the nested gifts had been to open. As I added a splash of coconut creamer to lighten the coffee and took a sip, another thought came to mind. God had nested His Christmas gifts to all of us too.

He wrapped His Son — His only Son and child of a virgin — in swaddling clothes to bring us the gift of salvation and eternal life. With faith to believe and receive His gift, we are also given His true and living Word proclaimed in the Bible, blessed assurance of our adoption into His family as children of the King of Kings, and the indwelling power and everlasting presence of His Holy Spirit.

I tucked my thumb into the handle of my mug and cradled the wildflowers adorning the freshly brewed coffee. As everyone headed back to the living room, I took a moment to pause and whisper a prayer of thanks for my husband, God's greatest earthly blessing to me, and his thoughtfulness.

Walking to join the family, lyrics of a familiar hymn of praise softly echoed in my mind: "All I have needed, Thy hand hath provided."

17

Finding Christmas
A Short Story

Barbara Culley

MARIE CHOKED BACK TEARS as the police officer questioned her. He seemed to sympathize with her sense of violation and loss, but that was little comfort.

Marie's coworker had propped open a back door which allowed the stranger to slip in unnoticed. Bolt cutters made quick work of two locks in the employee lounge before the thief was interrupted and fled. One locker had held a coat and a few paperbacks. Marie's locker had held her purse with the money she had saved to buy Christmas presents for her kids.

When the police finished their report, Marie's supervisor suggested she take the rest of the day off.

How's that going to help? she wondered. After her husband had died, necessity had driven Marie from her happy role as wife, mom, and homemaker. Given a lack of marketable skills and work history, she had been grateful to find a custodial job to support her family. She had scrimped through the year to make this holiday special. Now her savings were gone in an instant.

Marie returned to her housekeeping cart to continue her work. As she waited for a chattering group of women to exit the restroom she had been cleaning, she thought about how tight money was for her family of four. They lived simply, always praying no catastrophic event would occur. The meager reality would have been bearable but for her desire to give her children more.

"Failed again, Marie! Why did I bring the cash I'd saved to work?" she chided herself. "Because I bounced checks after Ted died and I'm on a list." Her internal critic was hard at work.

Her manager had already informed her that their employer would not cover losses from theft. She wondered if there might be another way to reclaim part of her plans. Maybe she could work some extra hours. If not, she would have to take another job part-time to earn back what had been lost.

Other than her simple wedding band, she had nothing of real value to sell. Her fingers caressed the symbol of her vows to the man she still adored. Since he died life had been a struggle not only to make ends meet, but also dealing with the emotional impact. The family was more stable now, but this blow was a setback. It felt like much more than money had been stolen.

The strong scent of perfume floating down the hall toward her told her the women were leaving the restroom.

"Back to work, Marie," she told herself, steeling her heart against the sadness threatening to overwhelm her.

At lunch she followed up on her ideas to work extra hours or take a part-time job to make up some of the missing money. She asked about overtime, but none was needed. Stores she contacted had already hired personnel in preparation for seasonal shopping.

"Well, that's that," she thought.

Marie finished her shift, feeling her heart grow heavier by the minute. She dreaded telling her kids about the theft, but hoped it would help them understand the need to tighten their budget . . . including for Christmas. She silently rehearsed her message focusing on thankfulness that no one was hurt, and the true meaning of the season. Her throat tightened at the mental image of her children's sad faces. She breathed a quick prayer, turning to her constant source of strength. "Father, please help me."

After dinner, Marie led her kids to the living room. As she shared the troubling events of her day, cries of shock and dismay filled the air. She reassured the children that she was fine and then explained the impact to the family's Christmas plans. Silence fell. Tears trickled from the eyes of her two youngest children. They fled to the comfort of her arms.

Marie watched as her eldest, Ricky, shook his head and squared his shoulders. Jaw tightening, he transformed from a boy to a young man before her eyes.

"It's okay, Mom," Ricky said, sitting on the coffee table to face the trio. "You're okay and that's all that matters."

Marie smiled, and nodded in agreement. "You're right, honey. We have each other, a roof over our heads, and food to eat. Remember, Christmas is about the birth of Jesus, not all the glitter and presents."

"But, Mom," her youngest said.

"Baby girl, I love you all so much. I'm sorry this year will not be what we had hoped, but we have each other. We will be fine. Ricky said it. It will be okay. I know it hard now, but we'll get through this . . . right, kiddos?"

They nodded reluctant agreement, not convinced.

Marie looked at her son. "Thanks, Ricky, for helping us think about what we have, not what was taken. Maybe we should pray for the man who stole my purse."

They bowed their heads in prayer.

The next day several of Marie's co-workers gave her small gifts of money and candy for the children. She knew each one of them had limited budgets themselves, especially at this time of year. She felt a balm to her aching heart from the acts of sacrifice.

After work she lingered at her front door, and fiddled with keys as she tried to reset her attitude before she opened the door.

As she entered the house, her eyes grew wide at what she saw — a Christmas tree in the living room and her kids standing nearby, their faces radiant.

"Surprise!" They rushed toward her.

Marie's heart swelled with unexpected joy. Life in the Pacific Northwest had its advantages, one being evergreen trees as part of the environment. This one likely came from the nearby woods. The tree was decorated with pinecones and holly sprigs added to the ornaments and lights collected over the years.

The scent of fir wafted in the air.

"Oh, my goodness! Look what you've done. It's . . . it's just beautiful!" They stood in a happy embrace. Marie looked to heaven with a thankful heart.

After dinner, Ricky said, "Mom, I've been thinking . . . ." Marie smiled. He had always been a thinker. "There's a family — the Martins. I know the kid from my class. Their dad left a couple months ago. Can we invite them over? I don't think they have much. Sammy and his sister seem so sad. I have a sweatshirt I only wore a couple times. I could give it to him."

"And I have Baby. I could give the sister my dolly," added her youngest.

"I have a game I haven't opened," her middle child chimed in.

"Oh, my darlings! Yes, yes, and yes! What a wonderful idea! Ricky, please do invite them. I'm sure we can all find a few things to give."

The days flew by. They found peace in their simple preparations for the holiday, and enjoyment in planning for the Martins to celebrate with them.

On Christmas morning Marie felt tentacles of sadness begin to wrap around her heart. She thought of the sparse festivities planned. She clenched her teeth. "No. Not today!" she muttered and banished the approaching shadows.

The kids joined her at the table with bowls of cereal. "How about hot cocoa, kids? I have whipped cream. Ricky, after breakfast, would you get the games out and turn on the music? Let's have fun and get ready for the Martins."

The lack of presents and a feast faded into the background.

Before long, a timid knock sounded at the door.

"The Martins!" They jumped up and followed Ricky to greet the family standing shyly on the porch. Marie and her kids ushered their guests in with warm greetings. The kids went to sit by the tree and play games while Marie chatted with Rita, their mom. The pleasure of sharing the simple celebration warmed the room.

"Thank you, Marie, for including us in your holiday. We've had a pretty rough patch. Money is tight with Bob bailing on us. None of us have been excited about Christmas," Rita said.

"Bad things happen. Trust me, I know. I'm sorry you are going through a tough time. But, it's Christmas, and we're so glad to have you here to share the day with—"

The sudden pounding at the door and booming voice of Marie's best friend's startled them all.

"What on earth?"

"Merry Christmas! What? You didn't think we'd be here? C'mon! Not happening." The woman pushed her way past Marie, holding a heaping platter of cookies. Three children trailed behind her, each carrying wrapped packages. "Hey, kiddos! Merry Christmas! Tom stayed home with the baby, but he sends his love. Oh, hello! I'm Gina, and who are you?" she greeted everyone with a wide smile. Marie's heart swelled at the steadfast kindness of her friend.

After everyone got acquainted, the children gave their presents to the Martins and then opened their gifts from Gina's family while the women chatted and enjoyed cookies and coffee.

A quiet knock interrupted their conversation.

It took Marie a minute to recognize the man standing at the door as the policeman who had interviewed her after the theft. He stood with a small group of strangers.

"Good morning! Merry Christmas! You may not remember me . . ." he began.

"Oh, yes. Yes, I do. Officer Riley. Merry Christmas! Uhmm . . .what are you doing here?"

"Well, I shared what happened to you with folks at my church. Some of us thought it would be nice to stop by after our own morning celebrations, so here we are. May we come in?"

"Of course. Of course!" She swung the door wide, still confused. "Come in, please!" Bewildered joy washed over Marie as a parade of food, wrapped packages, and smiling faces entered to join the party.

Marie served coffee and cocoa while the table filled with festive foods. Introductions buzzed in the air, and soon everyone was chatting, munching, and enjoying the holiday cheer. The children opened the presents and shared amongst themselves. There was plenty for everyone.

Over all the noise, the next knock was hard to hear, but the persistent sound broke through. Marie greeted members from her own church. News of the family's loss had moved hearts to action, resulting in more treats and gifts.

"How is this possible?" Rita's eyes were wide with wonder.

"Well, as I was saying, we've had our problems since my husband died, but our faith in God's goodness and caring has gotten us through some pretty dark days. Even now, there are times when I feel like a failure as a mom, but I hold on, knowing God is with me. I pray for His guidance and strength every day. God loves us. I'm sure of it. He is with us and He's for us, even when times are hard. God heals the brokenhearted. I know it. I've lived it. I'm still living it." Even with these truths on her lips, Marie felt overwhelmed.

"You know," she admitted, "I felt like I let down the kids this year. I couldn't make this the Christmas I'd planned, no matter what I tried. I was sad that I'd disappointed my family and that I'd failed again. But, look around. This is amazing! The caring and generosity of others are more than my plans and savings could ever do. The love of God spills over in people's lives and inspires them to care for others, just like today. I know you're hurting, Rita. Life can seem hopeless. If you would like, I'd love to have you and your family join us on Sunday for church. You may find the same peace and strength I have found in God."

Marie looked around the room. Happiness bubbled up in her spirit at the scene of friends, old and new, the cheerful chatter, and ripples of children's laughter. Her heart swelled with joy at the outpouring of kindness, a reflection of God's abundant love and best gift of all — His Son.

18

Scenes of Life

Helen L. Hoover

While I was at a sale, a counted-cross-stitch kit caught my eye. I bought it, hoping to finish it and then hang the finished product on our dining room wall.

The design shows a large angel in the sky with a banner: "Behold I bring you tidings of great joy. For unto you is born this day, a Savior who is Christ the Lord." The angel's large skirt is divided into six panels, each displaying a scene of Christ's birth: the city of Bethlehem, Mary on the donkey, shepherds in the field with sheep, angels singing, a manger with baby Jesus, and wise men on camels. The scene of an angel talking to Mary is on a billowing sleeve.

This intricate design has many areas to catch your attention. One of the angel's hands holds a dove sitting on its palm while the other hand holds a horn to the angel's mouth. Various colors of red, blue, green and yellow flow through the whole picture. Ribbons and tassels hang off the garment.

I soon realized this project would take several months to complete and I needed God's guidance to figure out how to do it expertly. I started by using black thread to divide the plain white fabric into areas for the different scenes. As I started each scene, I questioned God, "How can I possibly get this to look good? And where do I start?" I didn't try to work on more than one scene at a time. I concentrated on and finished each area before starting another one. Gradually the picture came to life.

The completed cross-stitch picture now hangs on our wall. I'm very pleased with it. There are some mistakes, but nothing very obvious. My husband made a wooden hanger to display it on.

As I worked on this hand-stitched hanging, I realized it was similar to my life. There have been many scenes and will probably be more as the weeks and years go along. I had to concentrate on each situation as I worked through it. At times, I wanted to escape, but that wasn't an option. I stuck with the sometimes-challenging situations, and survived.

I've had scenes of childhood, early marriage, raising children, job experiences, traveling, ministry, and retirement. In each of life's scenes, I've needed God's help and guidance. I've wondered how some of the situations could possibly work out for the good. But God was there with me through them all, whether they were fun, difficult, exciting, or mundane.

It is now an interesting life picture as I think back over the various scenes. I am thankful for God's continued faithfulness as I've navigated through this fascinating earthly life.

> *"I will lead the blind by ways they have not known,*
> *along unfamiliar paths I will guide them;*
> *I will turn the darkness into light before them*
> *and make the rough places smooth.*
> *These are the things I will do; I will not forsake them."*
>
> Isaiah 42:16 NIV

19
My Favorite Customs and Moments

Peggy Park

Over the years I have learned that certain things make the holidays more joyful.

For instance, when I was a child, our family always drew names for Christmas gifts. Today my immediate family includes eight adults and six grandchildren. As the family grew, I adopted this same practice. We've found it to be a big relief for everyone, especially after the children became old enough to draw among themselves. It has reduced the dilemma of gift selection and has made it a joy instead of a long list of names to work through.

Because our family members are in three different states, my daughter, Susan, has assumed the responsibility of drawing for each person and mailing them their name. She said she thought I was rigging the drawing so I would get the easier ones for myself and my husband. Of course, it was a joke but it certainly was tempting as some family members are harder to buy for than others.

Another helpful way I have found to relish the holiday is to focus on my good friends' birthdays throughout the year rather than putting pressure on myself to get each person a gift at Christmas.

We celebrate our birthdays with a lunch and perhaps a gift. If I come across something in my shopping that seems perfect for a particular friend I get it, but we don't expect gifts from each other.

For one family I know, I make little "goodie" bags for each of the four children and their parents, since they do not have an involved extended family. I invite the entire family to come for refreshments a couple of weeks before Christmas day to catch up on their lives and give them their gift bags. Often the gifts are little trinkets as well as spiritual items the mother may suggest. I hope this has a lasting impact on them.

I am not a "pull-out-all-the-stops" woman in regards to Christmas baking so I avail myself of various prepared foods and delegate some of the food preparation to those who enjoy it. At my son-in-law's suggestion we have a birthday cake for Jesus at our holiday meal. Singing "Happy Birthday" to Jesus helps us focus on the real meaning of the celebration.

As our children were growing up we enjoyed drawing names for what we called "Christmas angels." The purpose was to do nice things for the person whose name you drew without that person knowing it was you. It could be making their bed, leaving a treat on their pillow, or perhaps doing a chore that would have been theirs to do. It was a lot of fun on Christmas day to hear shouts of "Oh! It was you who did that!" as each person learned who had been their secret angel.

Over the years I have learned not to think I have to attend every program or event offered. I have also learned to lay aside my expectations of the "perfect" holiday, to slow down, and to be sure the activities do not usurp my time to be with, to celebrate, and worship the birthday baby.

But the most important way I have found to slow down and keep Christ central to the holiday is to come to Him each morning to fellowship with Him, worship and adore Him, read His word, and lay my burdens at His feet.

20

A Gift from the Sea

Lola Di Giulio De Maci

In grade school, I shuddered at the thought of writing that imperative after-the-holidays essay: What traditions does your family celebrate? What foods grace your holiday table?

Our teacher, her veil like a halo against the shiny, black chalkboard, would call on us to stand up next to our desk and recite what we had written. I always tried to make myself as invisible as possible, because I was not good at reciting anything in front of my peers, let alone sharing what our family ate for Christmas dinner.

One by one my classmates' stories unfolded:

"My mother cooked a honey-baked ham with mashed potatoes and green beans.

" . . . oven-roasted turkey with cranberry sauce."

" . . . a Christmas goose."

Ham? Turkey? A Christmas goose?

I soon realized that not everyone in the world had homemade gnocchi or lasagna for Christmas dinner. I hail from a large Italian family who loves food and loves to eat, but our Christmas dinner never had a turkey or a goose sitting on a platter in the center of our table.

When it came my turn to deliver my after-the-holidays

masterpiece, my voice disappeared somewhere into my body. I heard my words proclaim something we ate that was smothered in tomato sauce.

It seemed like an eternity and a day before I sat down.

Many Christmases later, Uncle Mike — my dad's brother from Italy and now living in Los Angeles — was coming for Christmas dinner and was bringing "a delicacy" to add to the holiday fare.

Finally, I thought, maybe a ham baked in honey; a turkey roasted in the oven; or maybe something even better, like an exotic Christmas goose Italian-style? I only wished I could roll back time, stand next to my desk, and present to my class an essay on what we had to eat on Christmas day, Italian-American-style.

The large, oval-shaped wooden table in our kitchen was set in holiday fashion. Mom's best plates and glasses were rescued from the China closet and washed and buffed until they sparkled like the Star of Bethlehem. Dad's homemade sausage and wine sat alongside the award-winning gnocchi (small Italian dumplings made from potatoes, semolina, or flour) in homemade tomato sauce. In the center of the table, the China platter awaited the honor of displaying the forthcoming Christmas special Uncle Mike was contributing to our holiday dinner. My heart sang: Bring on the Christmas surprise!

When the doorbell rang, my sisters, brother, and I scampered to the front door wanting to be the first to greet Uncle Mike and his "treasure." Perfectly concealed, the "treasure" had to be prepared and cooked before its revelation and presentation. What could it be?

After the piece-de-resistance made its procession to the table, I helped myself to this strange-looking food that sat quietly on Mom's prized platter. I didn't recognize it, but perhaps, I surmised, it was turkey or ham or goose disguised in tomato sauce. I chewed and chewed this munchy morsel, but I couldn't swallow it. It wouldn't go down. The texture was sticky and rubbery and oily.

I made a bee-line to the kitchen sink to get rid of it and rinse my mouth. And there, lying limply in the sink, was the head (an eye still intact) and the tail of an eel! A slimy, slippery eel! Uncle Mike's delicacy! I made my way back to the table where Uncle Mike sat beaming, believing that he had given us a special Christmas gift to remember.

And he certainly had!

Today, all these many Christmases later, I would proudly write my after-the-holidays essay in all capital letters, stand head-held-high in front of my classmates, and shout what I had had for Christmas dinner — especially the part about the slimy, slippery "delicacy."

I grew to realize that my parents spent hours mixing, rolling, kneading and shaping dough into delicious bite-size pieces of gnocchi in addition to chopping, dicing, mincing, and sautéing ingredients for a sauce that simmered on the stove for up to four hours. And they did it out of pure love.

I recall the joy and beauty of a family gathered around our kitchen table eating, laughing, sharing.

Maybe my classmates did have ham, turkey, and an occasional goose for their Christmas dinners, but I'm sure they would have loved to come to our house for a gnocchi dinner complete with all its trimmings. They would never have left our table wanting more. My mom and dad would have seen to that.

There was always plenty of good food and laughter to go around. Enough for an army.

I have never had eel again, with or without the head or tail, but I do have very sweet memories of an Italian uncle who came to our house for Christmas dinner one year and brought with him a Christmas surprise, a "delicacy," that I remember fondly as an inimitable, priceless gift from the sea.

21
A Sweet Wonder

Charlene Warren

Such a sweet wonder
Resting upon the hay.
This is like no other day
Before or since.
For we have seen the Prince.

Tiny now are His precious hands,
But one event in His prime
Will change them for all time.

Long and arduous will be that Calvary climb.
How could one, in this little manger,
Who's so sweet and tender,
Be put through such torture and pain?

Yet that sweet little babe,
Who knew no wrong,
Went to the cross where we belong.
Because He loved us so much,

We have but to receive His touch.

22

The First Christmas Gift
A Short Christmas Play

Majetta Morris

NARRATOR: One night, many Christmases ago, as the animals were all snug in their warm barn, they began reminiscing of years past. They thought of things they had done, places they had been, and friends they had met.

The Donkey said, "I remember one time, oh it wasn't a long, long time ago, but it was when I was just barely old enough to be ridden. I remember a special girl mother-to-be that I carried from Nazareth to Bethlehem. Her husband had to go pay his taxes, you know. I tried to walk so softly, but still, at times, she needed to walk. But I carried her most of the way."

DONKEY SINGS: Hee Haw, Hee Haw, He needed me
To carry His mother to Bethlehem.
We looked throughout the village
For a place to stay,
But only a lowly stable
Did we find that day.

NARRATOR: The Camel grumbled back at him, "I don't know why you think what you did was so great! I was the one that had to carry the wood to build the manger that the baby was put in after He was born. I did that before you even thought about going to Bethlehem."

CAMEL SINGS: Grumble, Grumble, Grumble, Grumble,
Grumble, Grumble, Grumble, Grumble,
I'm the camel that carried the wood
For the manger where He lay.
The wood was heavy; the road was long.
It was hot and dusty that day.
Grumble, Grumble, Grumble, Grumble,
Grumble, Grumble, Grumble.

NARRATOR: The Horse complained, "Well, if I hadn't given my manger, you wouldn't have had any part at all. Because it was MY feedbox that they used to lay the baby in."

HORSE SINGS: How can I eat with a baby in my feed box?
How can I eat my oats?
How can I eat with a baby in my feed box?
Now I gotta eat with the goats!

NARRATOR: The peacemaking Cow replied, "That's all right, Mr. Horse. I'm sure that the baby and mother appreciated your contribution. All I gave was a little sweet-smelling hay."

COW SINGS: I gave them my hay in which to lay
The baby in the manger.
It wasn't much, but was all that I had

	To offer to this stranger.

It was so fresh and smelled so sweet
The blades of straw would tickle his feet.
I gave them my hay in which to lay
The baby in the manger.

NARRATOR: The little Mouse squeaked, "Well, I wasn't there at the time, but my great-great grandfather was. He said that the hay was kind of hard. He said he had a difficult job making it soft enough for the baby to lay on. In fact, he said — so my father told me — that this was the song he sang while he worked."

MOUSE SINGS: I'm a little mouse hiding in the hay
Of the little bed where Jesus lay.
I chew, chew, chew to make it soft
In the little bed where Jesus lay.

NARRATOR: The Doves cooed, "With all the excitement of that first night, the baby had a hard time sleeping, so we turtledoves did our part, too."

DOVES SING: We sang a lullaby
To the tiny Baby.
Coo, coo, coo.
We sang a lullaby
To the tiny Baby.
Coo, coo, coo.

NARRATOR: The Rooster strutted around until he was sure he had everybody's attention. Then he loudly boasted.

ROOSTER SINGS: (LOUDLY)	Cockle-doodle-doo, I sang that morning To wake the little Christ Child. Cockle-doodle-doo, I sang that morning To wake the little Christ Child. Cockle-doodle-doo, Cockle-doodle-doo, Cockle-doodle-doo.
NARRATOR:	Everybody hollered for the Rooster to quieten down. One of the Horses reprimanded, "That's just what you did that morning — woke everybody up! After having late night visitors, too!" The Owls piped up, "Well, we were the Greeting Committee. Let us sing our special welcome song for you."
OWL SINGS:	Who, who, who are you? Is the song I sing. Are you the shepherds from the fields Who heard the angels sing? Come and see the Christ Child In the manger bed. He is wrapped in swaddling clothes As the Angel said.
NARRATOR:	Oh, it was a lovely night, this special night of our Christ's birth. Listen as all the animals join in with carols.

All the Animals sing "Silent Night" and "Away in a Manger."

(A Living Crèche Scene could be inserted here.)

[Adults, teens, or children dressed in Bible costumes enter as the animals sing to set the traditional scene. Joseph, Mary, Angels, Shepherds, Wise Men]

NARRATOR: The animals all felt so proud of themselves for what they had done. The rooster strutted around; the turtledoves preened themselves; the camel grumbled that he had not received enough recognition. Each animal remembered its special part, when suddenly the donkey looked over at the sheep.

The Donkey demanded of the sheep, "Hey, what did you do? You are so bashful; I doubt you could do anything!"

The sheep hung his head in shame, and this was his reply:

SHEEP SINGS: I had nothing to give,
Nothing that he wanted.
He came to replace me.
I was once important,
But He took my place
When He died on Calvary.
He is called the Lamb of God,
The perfect sacrifice.
He gave His life on Calvary
That all men might be free.

NARRATOR: Then all the animals hung their heads. First one, then another said, "I have nothing to be proud of.

> The baby grew into a man and gave up everything he had."

Jesus did give everything He had for you. This is the season of the year to remember that. Do you feel like the sheep that you have nothing to give Him? All He asks is that you give Him your heart and live for Him. You can do that right now by making the following song a prayer to Christ.

Prayer Song: Into my heart,
Into my heart,
Come into my heart, Lord Jesus
Come in today.
Come in to stay.
Come into my heart, Lord Jesus.

Note: This school Christmas play and has been presented in many formats. To request the music for the animal's songs, see author's bio for contact information.

23
Nearness and Belonging

Terry Magness

Living in a fast-moving, non-stop, information-saturated, virtual-contact world can not only be draining, but can also leave us bereaved of true personal connection. Pseudo relationships can be formed online, but eventually we will realize that something very necessary to our well-being is missing.

God made us for a safe, enriching, and close relationship with Him and with those dear to us. We need physical and emotional nearness and gentle touch from those we love.

A term used for babies who are consistently denied the security of loving arms snuggling them close, the comfort and assurance of a rhythmic heartbeat next to theirs, is "Failure to Thrive." The baby may survive, but often does not enjoy good health, does not grow as it should, and certainly does not flourish.

My husband and I have a small but beautiful family — an amazing son, daughter, daughter-in-law, and three adult granddaughters whom we treasure. For some twenty years we have been scattered from coast to coast, as are so many families. Jobs, school, exploration, expansion of horizons, and more contribute to this nation's dispersed family syndrome.

The Internet platforms available for real-time visual

communication have been a great blessing. To a degree they keep us connected. We see our loved ones' beautiful faces, hear their voices, and learn what is going on in their lives, but we are limited. Just as a prisoner can receive a visitor, hear her voice, see her face, he is yet deprived of physical touch and nearness. This kind of isolation is in keeping with his punishment.

Being close to those we love is a gift, a blessing from God our Creator. Drawing near to those we love — face to face, heart to heart, and in our mutual love for and yearning to draw near to our Lord Jesus — is the highest and greatest gift of all.

The week of December 2023 our family tangibly experienced this Divine gift. It was the first time as adults that every member of our family was able to come home and celebrate Christmas together. Ours is a high-energy family in which activity ideas generally fly like popcorn. Instead, the very first night a soothing contentment, a peace and tranquility seemed to wash over us all. We had fun, played, and lounged together, enjoying one another on a level like never before. Each seemed filled with love and appreciation to simply *be* and soak and rest in the loving presence of the family they love. A sense of nearness — yes, *belonging* — permeated the atmosphere. A great comfort and feeling of well-being that all is right and good, filled our hearts. No one wanted to leave the room.

The level of warmth, love, and comfort I felt was beyond words.

That Christmas changed me. I believe it changed us all. We were privileged to step into a depth of nearness and belonging beyond what we had known or understood. For me, it was humbling. I could only bow my head in prayer. I thanked my Abba Father for giving each of us a refreshing and satisfying drink of His *father love* and for affording us a glimpse of His glory. The afterglow of His generous grace those few days we were together has never left me. Often, even to this day, I remember that special Christmas and His priceless gift to us, especially when He allows me to experience that same sweet nearness, the knowing that I belong to Him — and I give thanks.

24

I Have It All This Christmas

Lauri Lemke Thompson

It's Christmastime again, and a vast array of holiday music is seeping into my psyche. I love Christmas but the season brings me times of sadness as I contemplate what's missing in my life.

Missing? Yes, there is a long list of things I do not have that the season's songs lead me to believe I should have.

I have no figgy pudding.

Or chestnuts roasting.

Nary a yule log.

Three ships sailing into my harbor? Nope.

No sleigh ride.

Not even the chance of drifted snow in which to take that sleigh ride.

The tune "Santa Baby" hints that I should expect diamond jewelry and a new car.

Not going to happen.

Much more seriously — and thus the triggers for true sadness — many lyrics assume I have loving family members and dear friends hanging from the rafters, filling my home with laughter.

Well, I simply do not have that, either.

Getting misty-eyed for me? Don't. I finally realized that perhaps I was tuning in a bit too frequently to all those popular Christmas songs. For me, everything changed when I switched the radio station and started listening to songs about the Bethlehem Baby and Who He grew up to be, for me and for you.

Guess what? No more pity party!

Suddenly I realize I lack nothing. I have everything I need to make this Christmas season wonderful.

Do I sometimes wish for a bevy of folks gathered at my yuletide fireplace? Sure. If you have that, by all means embrace it and thoroughly enjoy it.

I am not forlorn because what I do possess is the precious truth of Jesus' coming to earth to become my Savior, and the knowledge that He is the soon-coming King. I treasure all that means for my present and my future.

I could not be more richly supplied. My cup runs over with the many things I have, such as forgiveness and salvation.

The opportunity to fellowship with, trust, and serve God is also mine — to say nothing of a forever home in Heaven.

How incredible!

I also have plentiful opportunities to serve and give to others, some of whom have far less than I have. It's no secret that such generosity can bring bountiful joy to the giver.

To quote the classic hymn "Great Is Thy Faithfulness," I have "blessings all mine and ten thousand beside!"

We sometimes hear Christmas shoppers commenting, "I don't know what to get her. She has everything."

Well, I now feel like that person who indeed has everything.

I've learned that I just have to change the station every now and then.

How about you? Are you tuned in to less-than-helpful voices? No matter the time of year, try "switching the station" and you will be amazed at the results.

25

The Nativity
Which One Are You?

Kathy Tharpe

Snow began to fall right on schedule as I began to set out my traditional Christmas decorations. We have moved eighteen times over the years. In addition to three different areas in Germany we have lived in Alabama, Texas, North Carolina, and back to Kentucky three times. I have collected a Polish cornsilk Holy Family, a clay Nativity set from Mexico, a simple contemporary Holy Family from Germany with a smooth wooden surface and no fancy decoration, a baby Jesus in a walnut shell from the Ukraine, and a set of burlap Holy Family dolls from our German landlord's wife, complete with her husband's handmade Alpine chalet crèche.

My granddaughters came out to "help" Nana set up her tree.

"Now, Nana is very particular how she sets up her tree," their mother warned.

Huh? Isn't everybody? I mean, there is a certain hierarchy involved, isn't there?

Then I remembered how my boys, when little, stuck all the ornaments in a two-foot circle at their eye level and considered the job done. So I considered that a short briefing might be in order.

"Okay, all the stars go at the top of the tree, lighting the way to baby Jesus; then all the angels and angel bands heralding his arrival; followed by all the little babies representing all the different countries. Then come the nutcrackers, the guardians: some chubby, some skinny and some with actual working mouths. The collection of Santas come next and then around the bottom is a collection of painted elves from Germany that are there to guard the presents."

The two girls listened patiently and then ran off to play. I felt like Grandma had just sucked all the fun out of Christmas. But don't the stars, angels, and Jesus belong at the top?

Later, alone, I set my wooden arch from Germany — with its little wooden figures representing the nativity scene — in the window. A timer would automatically click the seven electric candles on at dusk and off at bedtime every day until Christmas.

I bent down to study the simple figures on the piece of wood underneath the arch. Each of them faced the manger in the center.

Where was I represented in that scene?

Surely I was Mary, the only woman present, kneeling reverently looking something like a princess with her long headdress. But am I Mary, the most holy of women who found favor with God?

Quickly moving on, I considered poor Joseph, all set to marry Mary. She goes to visit Elizabeth for three months and comes back visibly pregnant. An angel appears, tells him not to fear taking Mary as his wife and that she will give birth to a son who will save His people from their sins. (Matthew 1:21) That's something that doesn't happen every day. Imagine how trusting of God Joseph had to be —living in a proud, male-dominated society — to stay with Mary, a pregnant virgin whom he had grounds to divorce from their arrangement. Both faced ridicule, scorn, and whispers.

How steadfast their faith was to an unseen God!

Maybe I'm more like the wise men. I like to think I'm wise. They recognized the signs that someone special had been born and came on a vast journey to worship Him. (Matthew 2:2) We portray them as kings bearing gifts. Did they give out of their wealth, maybe a tenth of their treasure, or did they give just a token to a baby lying in a manger? With my time and talents do I give the Lord my best, or the scraps?

Perhaps I'm like the angel going out to the shepherds to proclaim the good news. Do I do that? Am I a messenger going out to share the good news of Jesus with others? Well, to be honest, I'm kind of shy and don't like to be challenged.

Or, am I like the shepherds, eager to go see for myself, leaving behind the flock that has been entrusted to me? How many times do people actually hear angels proclaiming to them? That must have been pretty exciting. But wasn't it kind of irresponsible, to run off and leave their sheep with no one to protect them?

Hopefully, I'm not the sheep. They're not known for their intelligence. They tend to wander off and can become highly excitable. Still, the smart ones stay by their shepherd. And if the Lord is my shepherd, isn't that the safest place to be . . . near the shepherd?

There's one more figure in my set. A man approaches the manger with a walking stick in one hand and a string leading to a camel in the other. The string is taut and the camel is carved at such an angle that his defiance is apparent. He strains not to proceed. The man comes perhaps curious, hearing the story from the shepherds or the angels. But the camel is dragged, his legs stiff with rebellion. The struggle is apparent. Man to beast, like parent to child or spouse to spouse . . . or my will to God's will.

I'll never look at my simple little nativity set in the same way again. It's like a mirror, because now I see myself in all the figures.

I am Mary in her headdress, chosen by God.

I am Joseph, not always understanding but obedient and learning to trust God.

I am the wise men coming to worship and give of my wealth, my time, and my energy, not just my spare change.

I am the angel proclaiming the good news with a bumper sticker, a cross around my neck, my behavior, or an encouraging word to friends and strangers alike.

I am the shepherds, eager to see my Lord.

I am the sheep, staying close to my shepherd.

And unfortunately, sometimes I'm that hard-headed camel learning to bend my will.

A Different Kind of Christmas

Norma C. Mezoe

After my husband became a Christian in 1970, the way our family observed Christmas changed. On Christmas Eve, we dimmed the lights, lit candles, and listened to a Perry Como record as he sang Christmas carols and recited verses from the Bible detailing the birth of Jesus Christ. Then, my husband led in prayer.

The years passed quickly, and our three children became young adults. During those years my husband had become a part-time minister and in May 1981, he was called to become a full-time minister. We rented our home to a family and moved into the parsonage belonging to the church to which my husband had been called.

The year 1981 was the first — and last — time we celebrated Christmas in the parsonage. Our son was stationed with the navy overseas, so we were missing him. Our younger daughter and our older daughter, her husband, and their two children spent Christmas day with us.

Three months later our family as we had known it changed forever. My husband and a young wife and mother in the church where my husband was serving ran away together one Sunday at midnight. Unknown to me and our children, they had been having an affair. It had been going on that last Christmas our children would spend together with both father and mother.

Members of the church and others came to the parsonage to comfort me, but there were times when I ended up giving them encouragement. It seemed the Holy Spirit was drying my tears before they could form. I felt the nearness of his presence and it was as though I was being sheltered in his arms. Psalm 91:4 NIV encourages us with these words: *"He will cover you with his feathers, and under his wings you will find refuge; his faithfulness will be your shield and rampart . . . ."*

Many things changed in my life, including the fact that I needed to support myself. For the twenty-seven years I had been a wife, mother, and homemaker I had never worked outside my home. To complicate the situation, my husband had taken our only vehicle when he left, and I was stranded living in a parsonage located in the country.

A woman who was a member of the previous church my husband pastored came to tell me about a short-term job opening at a nonprofit organization where her daughter was secretary. The job would be for one month and pay minimum wage. I felt God opening this door and I applied for and received the position. Two days before the job began I was given a used car complete with license plate and insurance. At the age of forty-five, I began my first employment outside the home.

After I worked for one week, the secretary became unhappy in her job, and told the vice-president of the organization that she was quitting. She recommended me for that position.

That night, I toiled over typing a resume. Instead of listing places of employment, I wrote of the experiences and skills I had gathered throughout my years of homemaking and serving as a minister's wife.

I was interviewed the next morning and hired even though I had no previous work experience. I prayed silently throughout the interview, and I had the assurance others were also praying for me.

I began my job as secretary in March 1982, three weeks after my husband left. I had much to learn because we served seven counties, and provided services and gave free supplies to cancer patients who could not afford to buy them.

During those early months of work, I learned what it means to "pray continually." I had read Paul's two-word instruction in 1 Thessalonians 5:17 many times. Now, it was a necessity. Silently I asked the Holy Spirit to guide me in all the many things I needed to learn how to do.

The months raced by as I learned the many aspects of my job and became more confident in the work I was doing. My supervisor gave me good evaluations and pay raises. I was thankful for his patience and encouragement.

At times I felt the darkness of loneliness hovering around me, but those periods were few. When I was tempted to dwell on what might have been and to have pity parties that no one except myself attended, I found that singing hymns and praying helped chase those times away.

December 1982 arrived and Christmas was approaching. I thought about the previous Christmas when the family gathered in the parsonage and my husband was present. What would this year's Christmas gathering be like?

By this time, I had left the parsonage and returned to the home where we lived before my husband accepted the fulltime pastorate. He had signed the house and furnishings over to me. My single daughter lived with me, and we began making plans for the family to spend Christmas with us.

In addition to my children, son-in-law, grandchildren, and my parents, I included my former mother-in-law with whom I had a close relationship.

My daughter and I prepared a variety of traditional foods, complete with turkey and all the trimmings, plus ample homemade goodies. Santa even passed by and filled our stockings. For the first time in their lives, Mom and Dad received a stocking filled with surprises. We read the Christmas story from Luke 2 and everyone enjoyed being together.

It was a different kind of Christmas, but it was one filled with joy, peace, and love. God's presence filled my heart and my home. The Lord met my needs bountifully.

You may be facing a different kind of Christmas this year. Perhaps your spouse has also left you or maybe your spouse or another loved one died during the year and your heart feels as though it is broken beyond repair. You may have a child who is wandering far from the Christian home they grew up in. You or a loved one may be facing a challenging health problem, or you may have lost your source of income. The list goes on . . . .

Whatever your need, the God who covered me with His wings of love offers that same love to you.

Have a blessed Christmas.

27

How Joseph Loved Mary
A Short Story

Madonna Pool

It is a cool brisk night, and the moon is casting shadows on the trees as their branches sway slightly in the breeze. I am feeling strange tonight . . . actually, that's not completely true. I'm devastated and feel betrayed and disappointed by what I have just heard, what Mary told me. Her words have stung my heart and left me confused and torn. My stomach is in knots. How do I respond to her revelation? What should I do?

My mind takes me back to the first time I saw Mary. The first time I saw her face I thought the sun rose in her eyes and the moon and the stars were the gifts she gave to the night. I loved her from that moment on.

But now this? How can I possibly keep this young woman as my wife?

Mary, my betrothed, has just told me she is expecting a child, and I am left full of doubts. How can this be when we have not yet known one another? I love this woman and have wanted her to be my wife from the moment I saw her. What will everyone think when they find out she is with child? Will I ever be able to attend the synagogue or read scripture from the scrolls? Will I be able to walk the streets of Nazareth and not feel the stares and whispers of others as I pass by? If I continue in this marriage, will I even be able to find work or provide for my family?

But if I don't take Mary as my wife, she'll be stoned to death.

Now, as I toss and turn in bed, my mind races with what I have been told. Mary says an angel has told her she is going to have a child, but not just any child. She is going to bear a son — the Son of God, the Messiah. I know Mary. I want to believe her. Yet how can it be? And, if this is true, how can I live up to this call? What should I do? How can I love and be a husband to this woman who carries the Savior of the world, the Savior spoken of in Isaiah? How can I care for her and such a child?

Oh Lord, I am not worthy.

Something in my spirit whispers, "Just let it be."

I think of my parents and all my ancestors who have been waiting, aching for the day, the moment when the Messiah will come. All of Israel believes the Messiah will come soon and free us from our bondage, our oppression.

Has Scripture not foretold this?

But now I'm to believe the Savior will be born not only to someone I know, but to my own betrothed. Mary, my love, a commoner like me. How can I, Joseph, a carpenter, possibly raise and be a father to this child, the Son of God? Am I dreaming or is this for real?

And a soft whisper says, "Let it be."

* * *

I finally drift to sleep, but it is not a deep sleep. I toss and turn and beads of sweat dampen my forehead like drops of dew. Suddenly I feel as if a bright light engulfs me, and warmth overshadows me. I hear a voice telling me not to be afraid but to trust and take Mary as my wife. "God will take care of the rest. Let it be."

I waken from my sleep and remember what has just happened. Have I dreamed? No, an angel of God has surely spoken to me. I feel different, a little odd, but calm, more peaceful. I know what I must do. I have to see Mary. I need to see her face.

I find Mary helping her mother, Anne, prepare the morning meal. She is radiant, yet timid, as I approach her. For a moment I can't speak. Then the words of the angel in my dream come forth. Mary smiles as she listens to my encounter with Gabriel, and she looks at me with complete trust. Her hand touches my cheek, and I gently place my hand over hers. She feels warm, and her glowing eyes tell me that she understands what I cannot say, "Let it be." She knows my humbleness, my unworthiness, my fear that was plaguing my heart to honor this call from God.

We hold our gaze for a moment, and then I say, "Mary, I now understand what you have told me. I trust you and even though I don't fully know what will happen, I do know that I trust in God too." I pull Mary close and we embrace, her head on my chest, her arms around my waist. We stand there in this moment, a moment of oneness, a moment of knowing something bigger than us is going to happen. And we "let it be."

And I remember again the first time I saw her face. I had felt my hands tremble and the earth had moved under my feet. Now I hold that image in my heart and will protect it forever. And whatever I must do, I will protect forever not only Mary, but the child within her womb.

Mary said yes to the angel Gabriel's message from God. Her simple response was, "Let it be . . . let it be done according to your word."

God's plan.

And now as this journey of loving this woman has just begun, I trust in God, in His child, the Son of God, and I echo Mary's response, "Let it be." For in these words, I will always feel fully alive and fully blessed.

28

The Gift

Helen L. Hoover

The gift is wrapped so lovingly, sitting under the tree,
With ribbon, a bow, and pretty paper.
The contents inside chosen carefully by the giver,
That hopefully will be loved and cherished by the receiver.

The right time arrives for the gift to be given.
It is handled carefully, so as not to ruin the wrapping.
Anticipation rises as the gift is brought forth,
For all want to see what is wrapped so lovingly.

The wrapping is taken off and laid aside,
its usefulness is done.
The gift is held up for all to see.
Oohs and ahs become the goings-on.

Now the receiver has to make a choice.
Will the gift be lovingly accepted and placed in high esteem?
Will it be used as the giver had imagined?
Or will it be rejected and put away, never to be seen.

A gift is never given to be rejected.
For much time, effort and thought is put forth
To get the right gift for a special person
To help them and make life have worth.

As gifts come our way this Christmas season,
It is our decision as to how we receive them.
For once the gift is passed to us, the choice is in our hands.
The giver's part is over; he's done all he can.

The gift of Jesus Christ was given long ago,
By a God who wants to help us and loves us so.
Will we accept this gift to be a part of our life
Or will we set Him on the shelf and reject Him with a "No."

The gift God gave us was meant for our good.
Peace, joy, forgiveness, everlasting life is there if we will take it.
But a gift is never forced upon someone
The choice is ours whether or not to receive it.

For God so loved the world, that He gave His only begotten Son,
That whosoever believeth in Him should not perish,
but have everlasting life.

John 3:16 KJV

29
Three Special Gifts

Amannda Gail Maphies

When the Magi we read about in Luke Chapter 2, presented the Christ child with three rare gifts — gold, frankincense, and myrrh — what did each symbolize? Had these men expected a royal and noble birth when choosing these thoughtful, expensive presents? Were they surprised when they found a young child living in a common home instead of a palace?

The irony of a king, which brings thoughts of wealth, power, and affluence, being born in such a lowly environment, blanketed in poverty, danger, and unexpected conditions is enough to make one scratch one's head with confused delight.

While shopping with my mother at a flea market recently, I found three glasses that fit my idea of "vintage Christmas" perfectly. Yet, I talked myself out of them. I didn't need them. I certainly didn't have room for them. They simply were not necessary.

I walked into my kitchen yesterday and found those delightful vintage glasses sitting on my counter, along with a hand-written note from my mother. She had bought them as a gift for me. She knew I didn't need them, yet she wanted me to have them because she knew the spark of joy they would bring every time I use them or provide them to special guests at my festive holiday table.

The thing about gifts is, they are not necessary. But, *Oh!* the joy they bring! Each treasured gift arrives with a unique love language all its own. The excitement of knowing someone thought you worthy enough for them to purchase something special just to show they care — *that* is the real gift.

I am not sure what became of the gifts the Magi presented to the Christ child. Did Jesus' parents carefully pack them away for use at a later time? Wouldn't warm and cozy clothing or something similar for the precious baby have made more sense?

Gifts are not defined by *sense*, are they? They are given to bring a smile, a spark of excitement, warmth, and true enjoyment. Some gifts may be considered excessive, but isn't the old adage "It is better to give than to receive"?

Perhaps for the Magi, the gifts they brought were less about providing a perfectly usable trinket for the birth of our savior, and more about an offering of grandeur, respect, awe, and reverence. After all, even though perhaps unknown to them, each of their gifts was significant in symbolizing an aspect of the baby's future life — gold representing His kingship, frankincense representing worship and His deity, and myrrh representing His death and mourning — is there really a gift worthy of the child who would give His very life to save the world? I think not.

Going into the Christmas season, whether you are shopping for others or graciously receiving, whether you are falling in love with the absolutely perfectly-chosen present, or silently planning to re-gift something at the next holiday affair, keep in mind that all gifts are a symbol. A symbol of appreciation, love, and loyalty. The giver likely spent precious time pouring over the vast expanse of options, to find that perfect parcel just for you. Whether they hit the bull's eye of your heart or missed the mark by a mile, thoughtfulness is key to not only receiving with gratitude but also giving in love.

Just as those wise men gave over two millennia ago. Just like my mother gave me. Just like God gave us when He gifted the world with His own perfectly precious son in the form of a human babe birthed in lowly conditions yet shining brightly against the darkest of night.

30
Big Red

Sherry Diane Kitts

"Come over to the tree. It's time to see what's in these fancy Christmas gifts." Rich summoned the family and brought along his camera to record the event.

He handed me the bulging one, and I pretended not to know its contents.

I teased, "Is this the plush robe I asked for?"

"You'll see." Rich raised his eyebrows. "Go ahead and open it."

He looked at me like he had a secret, but ever since our first year of marriage, Christmas gifts have ceased to be a surprise.

I recalled the time when I hid Rich's gifts in the back of our closet. He enjoyed pranks and called me at my office the next day to thank me for the slacks he'd found.

"Are they for me?" I heard a slight chuckle in his question.

"You shouldn't nose around in the closet. It's Christmas!" I didn't find his discovery funny, but Rich received great pleasure when he made me fuss.

I turned my thoughts back to the box. Sure of its contents, I ripped off the holiday wrapping. As I pulled back the tissue paper, I saw the expected robe. But there was a surprise — it was red. *Bright* red. The fluffiest, loudest, shoutin'est red robe of all times. Far from my preferred color wheel of blue or green. I didn't understand his inclination to purchase this red one.

I managed a weak smile.

"It's the only one like you described. They didn't have any other color except white, and I knew you wouldn't like that." Rich gave me a puppy-dog look.

I held up the fire-engine-red robe and my thoughts rewound to another Christmas Eve — when Rich's father, Jim, opened an unwanted present.

Jim had a boisterous personality, and enjoyed being in the mix of conversations. He liked to banter with his wife regardless the occasion. That year she thought he needed a new coat for Christmas, but he said she shouldn't spend the money.

When Jim opened the package from his wife, he looked at her, and immediately tossed it to the floor.

"Take it back! I told you not to buy this coat."

She paid no mind to his shenanigans.

"Now, Baby." She stood her ground. "It was on sale."

I didn't want to repeat that Christmas scene or be unkind so I graciously accepted the robe of red.

"I like it, Rich. It looks warm and soft and the color's a good change." The thick robe with long sleeves and a rolled collar hung mid-calf.

He exhaled and flashed a wide smile. Proud of his purchase he gave it a name.

"I'm gonna call it Big Red."

Years later, on the eve of December 31, my mother left this earth for her heavenly home. It was as if I had suddenly dropped into a deep sinkhole. My chest felt hollow. Grief gripped my bones and tears left salty trails down my cheeks. In the nursing home hallway, I could hear people greeting each other with "Happy New Year." Outside, the night air penetrated my heart, and I couldn't shake the raw feeling. Not a moment about that night exuded happiness.

After returning home, I headed for the shower. I stood there and let the warm water cascade down my back. I shivered through the steam as a relentless chill hovered across my shoulders. I stepped out and spied Big Red on its door hook. After drying, I lifted it and slipped inside its plushness. Its sleeves wrapped around me like the hug of my mother's arms. The fleecy collar brushed my cheek like her kisses, and assured me I'd be okay. I imagined her soft hands and gentle laughter. I shut my eyes and recalled the scent of her perfume.

The New Year arrived cold and remained so throughout January and February. The robe and I became good friends. Its color brought me cheer and warmed my heart when I needed it most. I was so thankful I had accepted my husband's sweet gift, and glad I hadn't insisted on my chosen color.

Fast forward six more years, to a more joyous night in December. Rich and I trekked through Epcot at Disney World to attend a Christmas musical, and enjoyed the beautiful performance. Exhaustion overtook us as we walked around the park, and the next morning my joints ached. I meandered through my daily routine, and decided to relax outside in the backyard.

Yes, I wore the red robe.

I pulled it around me and stretched out on the chaise. The sun gleamed against the backdrop of a robin-egg blue sky. A small breeze tinkled through the wind chimes. Honking Sandhill cranes flew overhead while a jet high above them painted a silent white stream.

Rich came home from work and greeted me in the yard.

"Why are you wearing Big Red?"

"I needed a little comfort," I said, "but I'll get dressed for dinner."

As I walked to my closet, I paused for a moment and gazed into the hallway mirror. After many years, some of the robe's fluffiness had diminished, but its gift of love had extended far beyond my expectations.

God knew exactly what I needed, and He knew it had to be red.

31

He Became

Bob LaForge

I was watching the devastating effects of prolonged war and famine on people in another country. It was a terrible tragedy, and I felt pity for those who were experiencing it. I sat there wishing I could do something significant to help them, but the best I could think of was to pray for them and send money to an organization that helped them. All of that from the comfort of my living room. Not insignificant, but still . . . distant.

That is not God. God does not sit at a distance on His throne and shake His head saying, "Those poor, poor people" and leave it at that. God does more than feel pity for us.

He became.

He became a baby to common parents in a small, dusty Middle Eastern town. *Behold, the virgin shall be with child and shall bear a Son, and they shall call His name Immanuel, which translated means, "God with us"* (Matthew 1:23 LSB). He did not step into our world as a grown and powerful man commanding respect. He was born needy, vulnerable, dependent on humans for food, warmth, comfort, and love. How opposite to the One who created all things from nothing and who holds all things together.

He became a human and lived a life surrounded by the lame, the sick, the blind, the oppressed, the poor. *Large crowds came to Him, bringing with them those who were lame, crippled, blind, mute, and many others, and they laid them down at His feet; and He healed them* (Matthew 15:30 LSB). He was not oblivious to the suffering so that His life would be more comfortable. Rather, He went to where those who were broken lived and begged. He walked dirt roads. Not to judge. Not for a photo shoot. But to comfort, to heal, to be with us.

He became the Man of Sorrows. *He was despised and forsaken of men, A man of sorrows and acquainted with grief; And like one from whom men hide their face He was despised, and we did not esteem Him* (Isaiah 53:3 LSB). Mocked. Punched. Whipped. Crucified. Murdered.

He became our sin. *He made Him who knew no sin to be sin on our behalf, so that we might become the righteousness of God in Him* (2 Corinthians 5:21 LSB). Jesus became the worst of us so that He might cover that worst in each one of us with His righteousness.

He became the Lamb of God, slaughtered, that we might be brought to God. *It is a trustworthy saying, deserving full acceptance, that Christ Jesus came into the world to save sinners, among whom I am foremost of all* (1 Timothy 1:15 LSB). In one moment in time, every sin from every person who ever lived or who will ever live was crushed upon Jesus so that He might suffer the total of the Father's wrath at once.

He became the resurrected Savior. *Jesus said to her, "I am the resurrection and the life; he who believes in Me will live even if he dies"* (John 11:25 LSB). He became life so that we who were spiritually dead might be raised up to eternal life.

At Christmas we give gifts to bring joy to others. And, in

doing so, we bring joy to ourselves. God did not just give us a gift; He became us. He came to us, was among us, healed us, and died for us. And still today, He comes right up to the suffering and says, "What do you want Me to do for you?"

Surveys have asked teens what they want the most. You would expect answers like a car, lots of money, the best smartphone. But what ninety percent of the teens said they want most is quality time with their parents. Not costly gifts. But to be with their parents.

God created us with an overwhelming desire to be with others . . . and that includes Himself.

When we pray, we probably ask for "things." A better job, a spouse, good health, and so on. Our prayer requests can resemble a Christmas list, especially when we have a picture of God standing "over there" and handing us what we ask for. But what we need more than anything is the presence of God. He does not want to stand "over there" and hand us things. He wants to stand right next to us, put His arms around us and say, "I'm right here."

The One who holds all things together became the weakest.

He who sits upon a throne surrounded by angels saying continuously, "Holy, Holy, Holy" became a man surrounded by the poor, the forsaken, and those who yelled, "Crucify Him!"

The Man of Sorrows has become the God of all comfort.

I certainly cannot be there for every person who is lonely, hungry, homeless, or suffering. I can pray. I can donate. I can even travel to an afflicted area and help out for a limited time. Those are all good, necessary, and beneficial gifts.

But God is never distant. He comes beside us and gives us Himself. His availability is not limited to time or location. And with His presence we have grace, comfort, support, and hope.

32

The Gift That Hit the Right Note

Ellen Fannon

After sixty-eight Christmases, many of them run together in my mind, making it difficult to single out one particular year. But one thing remains the same. Each year, it becomes harder and harder to find a perfect gift for my husband, Doug. Or even a so-so gift, for that matter. After being married for so long, there is simply nothing left with which to surprise him. Even if I miraculously manage to come up with a good gift idea, Doug invariably goes out two weeks before Christmas and buys himself the item I was anticipating surprising him with. However, the one Christmas that stands out from the rest is the year I bought him a violin.

Doug, who has no musical ability whatsoever, had regaled me for years about how he took violin lessons in the fourth grade and how much he loved the violin. It finally dawned on me as to the perfect Christmas gift. Not only would I buy him a violin, I would also throw in lessons. I began my quest to obtain a violin, which was no easy feat, as there were no music stores close to where we live. I called around and finally found a music store about an hour away with a violin for sale.

In addition to going out two weeks before Christmas and buying himself the very thing I had planned on giving him, another one of my husband's exasperating habits is becoming overly nosy around the holidays. He monitors credit card purchases and asks questions that are better left unanswered, so sneaking away for several hours in the afternoon to purchase a violin was easier said than done. Nevertheless, I managed to buy the instrument — in cash so as not to leave a paper trail — and bring it home.

Then, the problem arose as to where to hide it. I didn't want to put it in our cedar closet, where I hid things for the kids, because Doug was always in and out of there. Even if I wrapped it and placed it under the tree, a violin case has a distinctive shape and would be easily identifiable. Then, the brilliant idea came to me: I would hide it in plain sight. He'd never notice. I wrapped the violin and put it on the shelf in our downstairs bathroom. Sure enough, he walked by the gift every day without seeing it.

On Christmas morning, he was stunned when he opened his present. I had managed to find the perfect gift that he would never have imagined. He fiddled with his new violin (pun intended) and tested out the bow, the rosin, and the strings. After the holidays, he set up times for his lessons. He dutifully practiced every day, much to the horror of our cats. Whenever he took the violin out of its case, all three of them — including the deaf one — ran for cover. I suppose they thought my husband's musical musings sounded too similar to one of their own being skinned alive.

Doug's fascination with his violin lasted maybe six months. After that, he became too busy to practice. He has since admitted that he likes the idea of having a violin more than the reality of playing it. The violin has sat in a corner of our bedroom, gathering dust for several years now. Still, despite its lack of use, I believe the violin was the best Christmas present I ever got him (and not one he went out and bought for himself).

33

Fragrance of Memories

Iris Long

Scott surprised me with a special gift our last Christmas together: Tresor. Though I had seen it as a familiar display on cosmetic counters in fine stores, I had never used this fragrance. Chanel No. 5 had been my favorite for several years. I wore Chloe, Shalimar, or Romance on special days.

Sniffing the opened bottle, I thought the scent was slightly heavy. But being careful not to display any disappointment, I held my initial impression to myself and applied a few dabs to my skin.

A short while later Scott asked me what I thought of the fragrance. Lifting my wrist to my nose, I was pleasantly surprised. It was divine! I extended my wrist toward Scott and happily encouraged his opinion. He smiled with love and confirmed Tresor was my perfect match.

The lavish gift set from Scott included a large spray bottle of cologne, a small bottle of parfum, a travel roller bottle, a large bottle of body lotion, shower gel, and body powder. Every time I used one of these products I felt enveloped in love. I stretched out their use until they were finished, long after Scott moved to heaven. The large empty spray bottle remains packed away. Just a whiff of this fragrance instantly transports me back to that time, and I rejoice in the love we shared from the heart of God.

I have many memories attached to scents.

The sweetness of honeysuckle reminds me of the kids my sister and I played with as young children in Beaumont, Texas. They lived behind the house where we were staying at that time. We enjoyed hours of carefree fun with these neighbors.

My first perfume as a young preteen was Intimate by Revlon, a Christmas gift from Aunt Lucy. I also received body powder with a fancy puff and a new nightgown. I felt so grown-up the first time I sprayed some onto my skin. When I remember that scent, I also remember an aluminum Christmas tree decorated with red glass balls, and lit by a turning color wheel. I wanted to sit in front of it and watch the changing colors all night while Santa rescued Rudolph and all his toy friends from Misfit Island and gave them to loving children. For a few precious hours anything seemed possible.

The smell of melted butter and maple syrup triggers memories of the many mornings we ate at the International House of Pancakes before work because I craved pancakes during the pregnancy with my first child.

The precious scent of my babies was a fleeting pleasure, as children grow up and the scents change. I remember those times when I touch the skin of an infant, and I am thankful for the gift of motherhood.

Familiar smells in the kitchen invoke warmth, reassurance, peace, and confidence in tomorrow. For me they reflect the love of the preparer for those who will enjoy the provision. They also recall priceless moments of connection that are formed around the table where we gather for a meal or a snack or something refreshing to drink as we talk.

Our memories are threaded not only with scents, but also with sights, and sounds that can trigger both joy and sadness. As life is marked by peaks and valleys, memories are created in both, then stored as we move forward daily. In that way, we become a part of other people's memories, linked beyond the moment we are no longer a physical part of one another's lives.

Everything we do and say, each experience, has an impact into eternity.

May the memories we create today bring a smile to our face and peace to our soul, and carry a beautiful fragrance into the future.

34
Christmas Without Gifts

Diana Derringer

*Each of you must bring a gift
in proportion to the way the LORD your God has blessed you.*

Deuteronomy 16:17 NIV

My sister and I have not given each other Christmas presents since 1971. Are we mad at one another? Is this an ongoing family feud? Far from it.

As young adults we decided to forego gift-wrapped items, that soon break or wear out, for gifts with lasting value.

Earlier that year we married within three months of one another. We faced the usual financial challenges of newlyweds. However, we both believed in the importance of mission work.

Inspired by the story of a single female missionary who gave her life for the people she served, we wanted to give as much as possible to our church's annual international mission offering. Like those who initiated the offering, we longed for people in every part of the world to hear the message of God's love.

Years later, I opened a small package from one of my sister's sons. The card inside said his gift that Christmas was a donation to international mission work.

I cried.

As we see in Old Testament festival instructions and the teaching of Jesus and others in the New Testament, everyone can give something. We also read throughout the Bible that God values each gift, whether large or small.

May we daily thank God for the gift of love and forgiveness through Jesus. May we also continue to explore new ways to give consistently and sacrificially to share that gift with our hurting world.

35
Emmanuel's Song

(Sung to the tune of the Quaker "Simple Gifts")

Jeanetta Chrystie

Tis a story told for ages of how God came to earth
In the form of a baby, through a virgin birth.
How angels told the shepherds where our Savior lay
In a Bethlehem stable in a bed of hay.

CHORUS:
Praises to God, to our King of Kings,
Praise the Prince of Peace whom our salvation brings!
Glory to Almighty God whom we now adore,
Promised Messiah, our Wonderful Counselor!

As the shepherds came to worship and the angels on high
Sang praises to God, the Christ's Child's lullaby,
So lift we up our voices and join heaven's throng
As we sing Alleluia, Emmanuel's song.

CHORUS:
Praises to God, to our King of Kings,
Praise the Prince of Peace whom our salvation brings!
Glory to Almighty God whom we now adore,
Promised Messiah, our Wonderful Counselor!

36

The Legacy of Joe Bell

Beverly Robertson

When our church held its annual children's Christmas pageant, I loved watching a two-year-old who wore a hat that resembled a cow's head with horns. She rose from her place on stage with the other "animals" and wandered down the center aisle. All eyes were on this toddler as her grandfather led her back up the steps to her place next to another little one in a donkey costume with big ears.

The audience of parents, grandparents and congregants smiled as a little boy and girl portrayed Joseph and Mary. Shepherds, Magi, and angels surrounded the holy couple along with children attired as animals. A young boy and girl read the scripture. Interspersed between these readings, the congregation sang "Away in a Manger," "Come Let Us Adore Him," "Silent Night." and other beloved carols.

When the pageant was over, the proud church family erupted with applause. As the children sat on the steps to the platform and gathered around the pastor, he told them about another young boy that had attended the church many years ago.

> Joe Bell came from a poor farm family with many children. After the Christmas program, he was given

a sack with an apple and perhaps a few hard candies. As one of the few gifts he would receive, it meant a lot to him.

When Joe grew up he purchased a farm in North Dakota and made his fortune in the insurance business, some say in oil. Neighbors said he was a generous man. He gave gifts to the children in the neighborhood and treated them to movies in a nearby town. He shared his knowledge about how to save and invest money with the older children. Maybe he enjoyed helping these kids because he had never married and had no family of his own.

When he would visit our little white church — nestled between cornfields — that he had attended as a child, hushed whispers would resonate around the congregation, "Joe Bell is here."

Perhaps looking up at the stained-glass windows with the names of those who donated them, he remembered how he had received a gift from the people of this church. Whatever the reason, he decided he wanted to give back so other children could receive as he had.

Before Joe passed away in 1966, he donated a large sum of money to the church. Part of it was designated for those children and the children of the future. He also gave the church enough to purchase additional property and pay for a new parsonage. This home would house and entice new ministers to come to our community.

I listened to some of the older people reminisce with admiration, and I regretted not having known Joe Bell. His story reminds me that we never know how a needy child could grow up to be such a blessing.

I often think of the legacy Joe Bell left behind, and how much he must have loved our little country church.

37

Christmas Redemption

Vicki H. Moss

Twas the Christmas Uncle Jimmy said, "If I'd had a boy like that, I'd kill him." Several Christmas-light-gawkers driving through the neighborhood reported Brother *already* dead.

The beginning of this tale proved even more tragic:

Each year at Chistmas, our neighborhood had a contest for the "best decorated house." The winner was determined according to a vote. There were many non-working mothers with time on their hands in our neighborhood, and many of them were Garden Club members who — since they wrote the list — had first dibs from the Christmas songs each family would choose from to use as the theme to decorate their homes.

By the time my family saw the list, all of the good songs had been taken. The best were: "Santa Claus Is Coming to Town" — A no-brainer. Everybody had a fake Santa laying around — and "Jingle Bells" (a breeze).

The leftover Mom brought home? "Suzy Snow Flake."

Bummer. Who even knew the tune?

We held a family pow-wow.

Brother's idea: My three-year-old doll, Darlene, could play Suzy. Her job: Stand in the frigid snow by the "Suzy Snow Flake" sign. With a smile on her face.

"Great idea!" Mom said. "We'll change the foil color we normally use to present-wrap the door. That will also change our decorations up some."

"I'll nail fake Santa's sled and reindeers to the roof and we can throw some wrapped packages in the sleigh." Dad contributed.

"The mailbox needs sprouting greenery and singing bells!" Sis gushed. "The cedar and shrubs must twinkle!"

Brother snorted in glee because my favorite doll — my run-to comfort girl when everyone in the family picked on me and I had no one else to turn to — would be exposed to the elements.

I blurted, "No way!"

Everyone else jingled with holiday spirit while eating tangerines and nuts. The family cut a deal: I could bring Darlene back inside after traffic died down to warm her up until the next evening when all of the Christmas lookers began driving by again.

What would really pacify me? An acoustic guitar.

The year before, I'd penciled it on the Santa list. Santa had Alzheimers that year. I'd stormed back to bed. Sobbed. Wailed. Pillow-punched. And sobbed some more.

The jolly fat man had also failed to assemble my Barbie Dream House. The guy wearing the flashy-red suit didn't have the first hint of carpentry skills. Even while wearing coke-bottle thick glasses, he reeked of incompetence.

Santa had one last chance.

The deal about the use of Darlene for "Suzy Snowflake" agreed upon, we were all now ready to dream big.

Mother had been hinting for months she'd like to have a bottle of White Shoulders perfume.

Daddy was always happy with a stash of chocolate-covered cherries. Anything that topped those cherries was pure gravy for him. Much better than socks and underwear.

Brother? Who cared! Pondering long, I bought a canned hockey player puzzle. Wrapped it. Scribbled his name on the tag.

Cousin Charles arrived unexpectedly. Mother would have to think of something on hand to give to him since there was no time for last-minute shopping.

Christmas Eve found us rattling presents, sucking ribbon candy, slurping cinnamon-laced wassail, crooning along with Alvin and the Chipmunks, belting out, " . . . please Christmas don't be late."

All except Brother. Trust me, no one missed him when the front door had been locked for the night.

DING! DONG! Now, who could that be at this late hour?

Upon opening the door, my parents were faced with a stranger standing next to Brother who was trying to dust snow from his jeans. "Son!" the stranger said. "You okay? I thought you'd been electrocuted by the spotlight wires!"

Outside, Brother had been fake-dying, casting shadows against the neighbor's house so he could watch himself slowly die and fall to the ground, then snow-writhe while pretending electrocution. All this while automobiles turtle-crawled up the street ringing out snow chain music. After dying, he'd bounce back to life. To die all over again.

What Brother hadn't counted on, was someone thinking he really *had* been electrocuted. The poor motorist had thrown his car into park, leaving his family with the car door open while they shivered in arctic air blasts, while he ran to rescue Brother. Which caused traffic to back up from Tennessee to the Gulf Coast.

After the man was reassured that "it was only a game, I was just foolin' and practicing my dying skills" and the door was shut, the earth quaked.

"Son!"

How could Christmas get any worse?

Yet, it did. Christmas morning, Mom opened *four* bottles of White Shoulders. Maybe that wasn't such a bad thing. Now she had a lifetime's supply and our living room smelled more aromatic, adding to the tree, apple, and tangerine smells.

But then Sis opened a present that was a yucky-colored blouse.

Dad's underwear was too small.

Cousin Charles (the surprise visitor) unwrapped the extra box of chocolates Mother had on hand to gift him not knowing he wasn't supposed to eat chocolate because it made his face break out in zits.

My guitar? Electric. No amplifier.

Santa was a schmuck.

Suzy Snowflake? Simply a loser through no fault of her own . . . and left out in the cold.

And all of this tragedy happening while Brother sat on the sofa tripping unsuspecting passersby — yet somehow, always managing to either redeem or resurrect himself.

So much for the holidays.

At twilight however, I, the angelic chosen child, stood before succulent turkey and sweet potato pie and prepared to read Luke's version of Jesus' birth.

I was praying for my rapture right after the nativity story and mouthed a heartfelt "Jesus come quickly," because presents had already been opened and I'd been utterly disappointed.

Later, after the feast disappeared from the table, Brother worked on the hockey player puzzle I'd gifted him.

Uncles conspicuously strolled by on their way for their sixth helpings of chocolate and lemon pies while surreptitiously glancing over at the table and eying the hockey player taking shape.

I could hear their snickering before I saw grins.

Last piece in to the puzzle, there were no pucks! Maybe no one was looking for a puck . . . because Miss August looked nothing like a hockey player.

Hmmmm. The puzzle wasn't a sports puzzle but more like . . . a Playboy bunny puzzle?

All eyeballs turned my way and the looks said, *Is this revenge for Darlene having to stand out in the cold to play-act Suzy Snowflake?*

How was I ever going to live this down? And how was I to know about the puzzle? It had a hockey player on the outside of the can so I, um, *thought* it was a hockey player.

What a disaster of a holiday!

Mom took a break from the kitchen long enough to see what all the chuckles were about and made sure the puzzle quickly disappeared. For good.

Oh, and the best gift I received from Mom that year was only a raised eyebrow.

Looking back over the years, I recount the many Christmas mishaps, blunders and disappointments — and I wouldn't trade one Christmas memory for a bucket of diamonds.

And Darlene? After living to see many more Christmases she is now retired.

38
A Country Christmas

Peggy Park

Growing up on a cotton farm in Mississippi was quite an experience. Christmas was quite different to the way it is celebrated now with numerous shopping trips in person or searching online for the perfect gift.

We were a family of five children with very limited income generated by cotton and the numerous other things my father did to supplement our income. He even trapped mink to send up north for those, what were to me, disgusting pieces the fashionable ladies draped around their necks when out to lunch.

The only heat in our drafty country home came from fireplaces. Our father would get up early and get a fire roaring from logs he had cut and stacked for the cold winter days. My sister and I never questioned how Santa got down the fireplace to leave our meager gifts and consume the cookies and milk we left for him.

Christmas preparations included a tree our father and brothers cut down from the woods behind our country home. Its stand was a water bucket filled with dirt or sand. We made ornaments out of whatever we could find. They included paper chains constructed out of pages torn from the Sears Roebuck catalog or the occasional pieces of construction paper we got our hands on.

Daddy bought a huge peppermint cane from the country store and cut it up in pieces for us. We also had popcorn balls rolled in delicious maple syrup. Oranges and apples were also on hand. We used the roaring fire to toast marshmallows.

We had a happy celebration despite our limited resources. My sister and I received jacks and paper dolls as well as a cook stove or pots and pans. Sometimes a baby doll was in our loot.

Our church group sometimes loaded up in a truck or school bus and we went caroling. The farmers' wives would sometimes offer us hot cider and cookies after we belted out carols.

In one corner of the country school's auditorium, some of the men constructed a triangular wooden frame in the shape of a Chritmas tree. The more adventureous would mount it, and we had a tree made up of people who would sing carols. It never failed that someone got dizzy and had to come down.

We shared all we had. Those were happy days of sharing our gifts and being creative with our meager resources. The memories linger on and warm my heart.

39
Little Drummer Girl

Lauri Lemke Thompson

Sometimes when we serve at church or elsewhere, our service seems easy and requires little sacrifice. But then there is that day when it becomes challenging, and it hurts to complete our commitment. Maybe we don't feel well physically or emotionally, but we still want to be there.

So it was for me one December Saturday night. I volunteered at the Billy Graham Library in Charlotte, North Carolina. A month-long special event called Christmas at the Library drew massive crowds every year, especially on weekends. No entry fee was charged; it was our gift to guests.

Our offerings included Christmas lights, live music, carriage rides, a beautiful towering tree, a live Nativity, seasonal treats . . . and a clear Gospel presentation.

One night it was especially chilly, but not chilly enough to keep people home. Given the throngs expected that evening we were short-handed so it was all hands on deck, with both staff and volunteers working hard.

I was assigned to welcome people at the main door, and the stream of visitors seemed never-ending. I had a miserable cold. My throat was dry and burning. Because of the high volume of people, I had to shout to be heard, causing my voice to crack. My head felt heavy and swimming, and I was lacking energy.

One could argue I should have stayed home. But it wasn't one of those times when another volunteer could easily be shifted to replace me.

I felt so strongly that I should work that night that I prayed God would protect everyone from my germs. I determined to keep smiling and to greet each visitor as if they were the most important person to walk through the door that day.

So I kept on, praying, "Give me strength, Lord — and give me enough throat lozenges!"

I have often thought that as Christians it is difficult to consistently have pure motives and to focus on serving God. I admit that at times I had come to the Library primarily to "help out" the volunteer coordinator or the Guest Services Department. I wondered if at times it was more for me than anyone else, to fulfill a desire to feel good about myself.

But on that particular night — perhaps because it did physically hurt to plod on for six hours — I said to God, "Lord, you know what? I truly am doing this for You tonight." I also told Him, "I'm sorry, God, that I can't do as well as I would like. I'm having such a hard time making myself heard, but I really am doing my best."

So, what had I just told God? Two things: I'm doing this *for You* and I'm doing my *best* for You.

Then I heard it, above the din. A nearby choir was singing in the crisp night air: "I played my drum *for Him*, pa rum pum pum pum, I played *my best for Him*, pa rum pum pum pum, rum pum pum pum, rum pum pum pum."

That's it, Lord, I thought. Tonight I play my drum *for You* — and I'm playing it *the very best I can.*

A rare moment, a pure motive.

Then He smiled at me, me and my drum.

40
Overflowing

Desiree St. Clair Spears

I was a single mom, trying to support three kids on my own. Their father was in prison, and I received no child support. I barely made ends meet. How could I afford Christmas gifts?

Early in my faith, I studied the Scriptures on tithing. God's Word made it plain: *"Bring the entire tithe into the storehouse so that there may be food in my temple. Test me in this matter,"* says the Lord of Heaven's Armies, *"to see if I will not open for you the windows of heaven and pour out blessing for you until there is no room for it all"* (Malachi 3:10 NET).

I decided to take God at His Word. Even when it seemed I couldn't afford to give, I gave. My check to my church was the first one I wrote each payday. True to His Word, God came through — time and time again.

I remember one incident when I needed forty dollars to pay a bill but didn't have a cent in my bank account. Certainly I didn't want to pay it late. I stopped by the post office to pick up my mail. Flipping through the envelopes, I recognized my in-laws' address scrawled across the top of one and tore it open. A card with a note from my mother-in-law read, "I felt I should send you this." Tucked inside was a check for forty dollars.

Christmas was drawing nearer. I thought if God could do

this, He could make a way for there to be Christmas presents for my kids. I just had to trust Him.

As the days grew closer to Christmas, I began to get nervous; I still didn't have any gifts to wrap. Never before had I asked for help from a charity, but I decided to humble myself and do it. I applied for a few gifts from a local organization, then later I received a phone call from a different charity. It was Angel Tree, a program of Prison Fellowship that reaches out with gifts for children of inmates. A family had adopted my children for Christmas and would soon be dropping off gifts.

Thank You, Lord! At least my kids will have a few gifts under the tree, I thought.

"Go buy the kids some presents for Christmas," my mother said and handed me a check for a large sum.

My mouth flew open. I was overwhelmed.

Then I picked up the mail and opened an envelope from my in-laws. I gasped when I saw a check made out in the same amount as the one from my parents.

I opened another piece of mail. My eyes grew wide at the contents. A third check in the same amount, this time from my in-laws' church.

Wow! God, I didn't imagine all this!

After church on Sunday, my pastor handed me an envelope as I was leaving. I ripped it open as soon as I got in my car. Another check!

Then another came from a relative.

I had to laugh.

The day before Christmas Eve I got a call from the kids' day care provider. "Could you stop by? I have a few gifts for the kids."

When I arrived, she confessed, "I organized a toy drive among the other day care parents."

"What!"

She led me to an enormous box of wrapped gifts. "There's more. We also collected food for your family."

I was truly humbled, my heart bursting with gratitude, tears overflowing.

Christmas morning came, and my eyes scanned the living room filled with presents. Under the tree, on the floor, the couch, the chair. Not an open space anywhere. We had to pick up a few presents and place them in our laps just to make room to sit on the floor.

As I looked around at the incredible scene, gifts surrounding me on every side, I was reminded of the promises of God: *See if I will not open for you the windows of heaven and pour out blessing for you until there is no room for it all* (Malachi 3:10 NET).

Give, and you will receive gifts – the full measure, compacted, shaken together and overflowing, will be put right in your lap"(Luke 6:38 CJB).

The kids tore into the gifts, squealing with delight. When they opened those from the day care, I heard first one, then the other cry out, "This is just what I wanted!"

How could those parents have known?

But I already knew the answer. The same God who knew we needed a Savior knows just what we want and delights in lavishing His children with good gifts.

Yes, the Lord is a God who keeps promises. He did just what He said He would.

I know that full well. My heart is filled to overflowing.

41

Miracle in a Coat Pocket

Helen L. Hoover

"Do you believe in miracles?" my dentist asked me.

"Yes, I do."

"While I'm working on your tooth, do you want to hear a miracle that happened to my family?"

"Sure." He probably hoped to divert my attention from the drilling he would be doing on my tooth. It worked. I was fascinated with his story.

"When my two brothers and I were ages two, four, and six, my dad had difficulty keeping a job. He barely made enough money to buy food, pay the rent, and utilities. There wasn't money for anything else. As children, we weren't aware of this family problem. My parents didn't discuss the finances with us.

"Two weeks before Christmas, my mother realized they weren't going to have any presents for their boys. She beseeched the Lord, 'God, please show me how we can give our sons something for Christmas.' A of couple days later, as she cleaned the clothes closet and rearranged each article, she also checked the pockets for old tissues, gum wrappers, and papers. When she put her hand down in her winter coat pocket, she pulled out a twenty-dollar bill.

"Later when my dad came home, she told him what she had prayed and then found in her coat. Neither one knew how or when the money would have got into her pocket. Since she had asked God for help with Christmas presents, they believed that was what they should do with the money. They were able to buy each boy a toy and had money left for a special Christmas meal."

My dentist's mother hadn't told him about the twenty-dollar bill until several years later. She never did know how it got there but she came to believe an angel put it in her coat pocket. At the time, this was a faith-builder for my dentist's parents, and in later years it became a favorite story to share about God's goodness to them in a specific time of need.

My time at the dentist's office that day had been encouraging nstead of being filled with the usual dread. I left feeling uplifted and joyful for knowing a wonderful God.

God has various means to answer prayers. Each testimony is a special acknowledgment of His gift of love.

The Lord is righteous in all his ways and loving toward all he has made. The Lord is near to all who call on him, to all who call on him in truth.

Psalm 145:17-18 NIV

42
The Secret Gift

Gina Stinson

Generosity has nothing to do with the amount of money you have. My dad taught me that.

I grew up in a suburb of Atlanta, Georgia in the 1970s and 80s. My dad traveled as a salesman, and as his family grew in number and stature, he settled into a job at a local department store. If sales were good we had no worries. But if the economy took a downward trend, people stopped buying the luxuries of the day — TVs, VCRs, video camcorders. It meant life for our family could be feast or famine.

My mom was a stay-at-home mom. She worked hard in the garden, keeping a tidy home, and homeschooling us kids. She was an expert bargain hunter, coupon shopper, hand-me-down receiver and left-over masterpiece-dinner chef. Call it frugal, resourceful or cheap — she didn't care. She took excellent care of our family. So much so, that I doubt anyone ever knew there was a struggle.

It just so happened that my friends were mostly from the small church my family attended. I enjoyed friendships that were built around homemade baseball fields, above-ground swimming pools, Sunday school lessons, and basketball courts. Weekends were full of sleepovers and youth activities.

None of us knew how hard our parents worked to make ends meet. But it always seemed there was an understanding to share, to offer when you had extra, to ask when you thought there might be a need.

There are moments that God allows you to see something and that "something" sticks with you forever. I experienced such a moment around Christmas time when I was ten years old.

The church service benediction had been sung and families and friends were embracing and taking time to wish each other a Merry Christmas. My family always lingered — sometimes long enough that a light-hearted deacon or pastor wanting to get home had to flicker the lights on us.

That particular evening we had been visiting with a friend's family. My friend was one of five children. Her parents had been in ministry, but also worked hard to provide for their family through a family-owned carpet laying business. No one would have ever accused them of laziness. On the outside you would never hear a complaint. They were happy, content, and always serving others.

But sometimes things are different than they appear. My dad had a knack for discerning when people had needs. He was a watcher, a noticer. That Christmas Sunday he must have known something we didn't. During all the laughter and holiday spirit, I saw my dad reach into his pocket and pull out something. He folded it carefully and inconspicuously and just held it in his hand. I was curious. He seemed so secretive, so futive, so covert.

We moved toward the door saying our, "Merry Christmas" and "Happy New Year" greetings. Final hugs and handshakes were given and received.

There I was, keeping my dad's hand in full view, wondering

what he was doing. And then I saw him. He moved his right hand to shake my friend's dad's hand. He moved his left hand to put it on the other man's elbow, sort of quietly forcing him to take what he was being given. And there I saw it — a one-hundred-dollar bill. A knowing look passed between the two humble men and they shared a solid, manly hug.

A single tear slid down my dad's face.

I don't think I fully understood, back in 1982, what I saw then. But I do now.

You see, one hundred dollars back then was like a thousand dollars today. My family no more had an extra hundred dollars than the next family in our circle of friends. But somehow, my dad knew there was a need and, in a moment — when he could have put it away for a rainy day, bought another gift for one of his own children, or spent it on something for himself — he gave a gift of love in the form of a one-hundred-dollar bill.

Generosity has nothing to do with the amount of the gift. It has everything to do with the amount of love, compassion and sacrifice behind the gift. That Christmas, our family had enough. But our friends needed a little help, just a little something to make the load lighter. And my dad could do that.

What a gift of love!

That Christmas I saw a reflection of Jesus in my dad's eyes. I may not have understood it then, but I do now.

Sometimes a gift of love looks like generosity. Sometimes it looks like a tangible gift. Sometimes it looks like an embrace. But the truest gift of love always looks like a reflection of Jesus Christ, that sweet baby, who grew to be a man, our Savior.

There is no greater gift of love.

43
Christmas Afterglow

Nancy Aguilar

Lord, keep my heart tender,
And help me remember
The gift of Your Son
And all that He's done.

Though Christmas is passing,
Your love will keep lasting
Beyond twinkling lights
And cold, wintry nights.

The presents were fun
But now that it's done,
Faint embers are burning;
The calendar's turning.

Your wonder and glory,
The manger's sweet story —
Lord, help me remember,
And keep my heart tender.

44
The Gift that Keeps on Giving

Annette G. Teepe

One of my sweetest memories begins with a woman named Helen. She came as a babysitter to watch my brother, Marshall, and me while Mom and our new stepdad went on their honeymoon. I was fourteen years old, and my brother was eleven, so we weren't old enough to stay home alone for an entire week.

Marshall and I were a bit nervous about having someone we didn't know stay with us. We were already reeling from big changes in our lives. But Helen quickly won us over, as women have throughout time . . . with food! Helen enjoyed cooking and eating good food and made herself at home in our kitchen. One day she made us a great treat — the most amazing sugar cookies!

I was excited about these large, cakey cookies with icing.

"Helen, can you teach me how to make these wonderful cookies?" I asked.

She grinned, gave a big laugh, and said, "Of course!"

We spent hours bonding in the kitchen while she taught me how to make those cookies. She was patient and kind as we passed the time together.

Marshall helped too but he was more interested in eating than baking!

As the years passed I continued to make the sugar cookies. I gave them to bake sales for fundraising events. For Valentine's Day I colored the batter red and iced them with vanilla icing. At Christmas they became green and red with added sprinkles to make them even more special.

As my son, Alex, grew, I taught him how to make the cookies. In sixth grade, he gave them to his teachers for Christmas gifts. He carefully selected which shapes each teacher would receive — a mix of trees, snowmen, snowflakes, and stars. We didn't put icing on them because we wanted to stack them in special Christmas containers. Instead, we sprinkled decorations on them before baking and they sparkled with reflected colors.

We used different containers each year — ceramic platters, tins, plates — giving something that the teachers could keep as part of the gift. The best part, my fondest memory, is the huge grin on Alex's face as he was delivering the cookies.

As he moved up the grades, Alex's reputation preceded him! At school, word spread about the cookies and, as Christmas drew closer, teachers would ask if they were getting cookies this year.

Even after he went to college, we continued to make the cookies. Our neighbors and friends became our new fans of the sugar cookies.

When my son found out that his college girlfriend had never baked sugar cookies, he borrowed my mixer, cookie cutters, and a copy of the recipe, and taught his girlfriend and her family how to make and decorate them. Her family made it even more fun by turning it into a contest. He was thrilled to share his Christmas tradition with another family.

Baking sugar cookies continues to be one of our favorite

Christmas traditions. Alex and I enjoy the time baking together and the fun of giving the cookies away. The laughter, baking, cookie-covered counters, and fun of icing the cookies are all part of our Christmas tradition. He told me one day that he will be making these sugar cookies with his own children.

Helen has long since passed away, but I like to think that she can see us and knows that her kindness and love when teaching me to make these cookies has continued to be passed down to others. I imagine her in heaven, baking sweet desserts!

Thank you, Helen, for handing down a legacy of cookie baking and giving.

A gift of love.

Sugar Cookies

Ingredients

1 C. Oleo
1 C. sugar
3 eggs
1½ tsp. vanilla

3¼ C. sifted flour
½ tsp. salt
1 tsp. baking soda
2 tsp. cream of tarter

Instructions

1. Preheat oven to 425 degrees
2. Cream oleo and sugar. Add eggs and vanilla. Blend well.
3. Stir the dry ingredients together
4. Add the sifted mixture slowly to the creamed mixture.
5. Separate the dough into two equal parts and wrap in waxed paper.
6. Refrigerate at least 2 hours or overnight.
7. Roll the dough ¼ inch thick.
8. Cut into desired shapes.
9. Bake for 6–8 minutes.

Icing (Optional)

Ingredients

1 C. powdered sugar
1-2 Tbsp. milk or water
½ tsp. vanilla extract (optional)

Instructions

1. In a large bowl, whisk together powdered sugar and milk to your desired consistency. Use less liquid for a thicker icing.
2. Optional: Beat in vanilla extract or any flavoring you'd like, or beat in a drop of food coloring to make different frosting colors.
3. Spread icing over cookies while they're still warm but not too hot or the icing will melt. Allow icing to set up at room temperature. It will harden as the baked cookies cool.

Yields ½ C. icing (enough for approx. 40 cookies)

45
O Worship the King

Laura Lee Leathers

You have probably read the Christmas story from the second chapter of Luke many times. So much so, that perhaps it's just a habit. We are so busy from Thanksgiving to New Year's Day with family and preparations, we may neglect to look deep into the Scriptures to see what new treasures can be gleaned from the story of the birth of Jesus, otherwise known as The Christmas Story.

For me, as Christmas approaches, I've learned to ask the Lord to show me at least one new truth, and He has done that. One particular year, I wanted to learn about the visit of the Magi, the Wise Men, a story not included in Luke, but rather in the book of Matthew. The more I studied, the more I learned. As a result I realized that after many years, I was still relying upon the story I had been taught as a child, not what the Scripture states.

Let's start with the personal opinions we've probably all heard. Somewhere, the number three is attached to how many wise men there were, possibly because of the three gifts mentioned. Someone gave them names — Caspar, Balthazar, and Melchoir — because they were Noah's descendants. In reality, though, we don't find their number or their names recorded in Scripture.

A Brief History

History traces the lineage of the Wise Men to the time of Daniel. Some commentaries suggest their origin can be traced to Abraham (Genesis 12). They were part of the Medo-Persian Empire.

> *The Chaldeans answered the king and said, "There is not a man on earth who can tell the king's matter; therefore no king, lord, or ruler has ever asked such things of any magician, astrologer, or Chaldean."*
>
> Daniel 2:10 NKJV

The assessment is that the Magi were ancient people from a priestly tribe. They were Gentiles, skilled in astronomy (science) and astrology (superstition). Some theologians believe they learned of the prophecy regarding the coming of Jesus Christ (Daniel 5:11) from Daniel, himself.

Another aspect of the Magi is that they were prominent men with tremendous political power even through the time of the Roman Empire. Because they were called upon to provide guidance and consultation in various matters of state, they were considered to be "wise men." (Also see Daniel 4:7, 9.) They were also known as "kingmakers."

The Question

Jewish prophets had foretold a ruler of the Jews being born in Bethlehem. No wonder Herod was agitated to learn the Magi were looking for *He who has been born King of the Jews* (Matthew 2:2 NKJV). And again, according to history, there was grave concern over these men being a threat to Rome.

From the wording in the biblical text we see that even before they came to Herod the Wise Men had been asking people throughout Jerusalem their question. They were genuinely seeking Him.

Scripture tells us the Wise Men had seen the star in the east. One thing we do not see throughout the twelve verses in this passage is the phrase "they followed the star." Instead, we read *we have seen His star in the East and have come to worship Him* (v.2 NKJV).

The Star

> *I see Him, but not now; I behold Him, but not near; a Star shall come out of Jacob . . .*
>
> Numbers 24:17a NKJV

The Hebrew word for star is *kowkab;* in Greek it is *aster* (Matthew 2:2). It means "His blazing forth, His Shekinah glory." Throughout the Old Testament, the glory of God is manifested by blazing light. It was the glory of God which led the Israelites (Exodus 13:21), filled the temple, and hovered over the Holy of Holies.

We know from Luke 2:8-14 *an angel of the Lord stood before them* [the shepherds]*, and the glory of the Lord shone around them* (v.9 NKJV). Could this have been the star the Wise Men saw from afar? Notice in Matthew 2:7, Herod asked the wise men when the star had appeared. We are not told their answer.

We do know that Herod instructed them to go to Bethlehem and search carefully and let him know when they had found Jesus, because he wanted to go and worship Him, too. These words from a man who, when the Wise Men did not return, had all of the children in Bethlehem who were two years of age and under killed.

It's also interesting to note that Scripture tells us the Wise Men saw the star, but the scribes, chief priests, and others apparently had not seen it (v.3-4, 7). Were only the eyes of the Wise Men opened to see the star because they were genuinely seeking Him?

After hearing the king, they went their way,
and the star, which they had seen in the east, went on before them
until it came and stood over the place where the Child was.
And when they saw the star, they rejoiced with exceedingly great joy.

Matthew 2:9-10 NKJV

Matthew tells us the chief priests and scribes told Herod what was written by the prophet Micah: The Child would be born in Bethlehem (Micah 5:2, Matthew 2:5-6). But they didn't mention the star.

Yet, the star guided the Wise Men *until it came and stood over the place where the Child was* (v.9 NKJV). This blazing star led the wise men to Jesus like the pillar of fire led Israel toward the promised land. It was the reason *they rejoiced with exceedingly great joy* (v.10a NKJV). Also note that at this time Jesus was no longer a baby, but a child somewhere under the age of two (v.16).

In his New Testament Commentary, John MacArthur tells us: Though having had limited spiritual light, they immediately recognized God's light when it shone on them. They had genuine seeking hearts, hearts that the Lord promises will never fail to find Him. (See Jeremiah 29:13.)

The Wise Men approached the humble abode, stepped through the front door, and immediately came face-to-face with the Child, God's only begotten Son. Can you even try to imagine the joy, the awe, the realization that after seeking Him for months, they had found Him?

And what did the Wise Men do? They fell down and worshiped Him. Then, the Wise Men opened their treasures and presented the gifts of gold, frankincense, and myrrh.

Many people will read Luke Chapter 2 on Christmas Day. This year why not start a new tradition by setting aside a time to read Matthew 2:1-12 too, and ponder the story of the Magi from the east who came seeking Jesus, finding Him, and worshiping the Sovereign King.

And remember . . . He has come, and He is coming again.

Therefore, God also has highly exalted Him
and given Him the name which is above every name,
that at the name of Jesus every knee should bow,
of those in heaven, and of those on earth, and of those under the earth,
and that every tongue should confess that Jesus Christ is Lord,
to the glory of God the Father!

Philippians 2:9-11 NKJV

Prayer:

Gracious Heavenly Father, How we praise You for Your Son, Yeshua. We thank You for Your incredible love, Your redemption plan, Your mercy, and Your grace. We thank You for the way You draw men and women unto Yourself. We look forward to the day when believers from every tribe and nation gather around Your throne to worship You. In Jesus' name, Amen.

About the Authors

Nancy Aguilar's stories, devotions, and poems have appeared in *Clubhouse* and *Clubhouse Jr.* magazines, *The Upper Room*, *Heavenly Company: Entertaining Angels Unaware*, and other publications. When she's not writing, Nancy loves flower gardening and taking long walks on the beach.

Cindy W. Arora desires to encourage others from the Word of God. She named her blog and website *Reflections on Beauty* because every word she writes and every art piece she creates reflects His beauty. See His beauty at www.reflectionsonbeauty.com.

Cindy's devotions have been published in *The Christian Journal*, *The Bible Advocate* and others publications. Her book, *Chosen: Understanding Identity and Authority from Ephesians*, is available on her website or at Amazon.

Jeanetta Chrystie, ThD, PhD lives with her husband in Springfield, Missouri. Her parents moved in with them in 2021. Writing part-time for 40+ years she has published more than 850 magazine articles, newspaper and newsletter columns, short stories, devotions, and poetry. A few of her publications include pieces in *Christian History* magazine, *Discipleship Journal*, *Mature Years*, *Clubhouse* and *Clubhouse Jr.* Her work has been included in the *Chicken Soup for the Soul*, *Divine Moments*, *Short and Sweet* series, and books of poetry.

Jeanetta founded the Ozarks Chapter of American Christian Writers (OzarksACW.org) in 2007 and serves as its president.

Learn more at www.ClearGlassView.com. Connect with her on LinkedIn: Jeanetta-Chrystie and Pinterest: Jchrystie.

Rachael M. Colby has a heart for reconciliation and a passion to uplift those who serve in tough places. She writes to connect cultures' questions with Christianity's answers, inspire faith, and motivate.

An award-winning writer of articles, devotions, essays, poetry, flash fiction, and children's picture books, Rachael is a longtime member of The Jerry Jenkins Writers Guild and a protégé in the Cecil Murphey Mentoring program.

Her work has appeared in *Chicken Soup for the Soul*, the Blue Ridge Mountains Christian Writers Conference blog, online publications, anthologies, and the *Oak Ridger* newspaper.

This Jamaican-born wife, mom, beach bum, artist, work in progress, makes her home in Cape Cod, Massachusetts. She runs on copious amounts of coffee, chocolate, and a whole lot of "Help me, Jesus."

Barbara Culley, a transplant from Nebraska, has lived in the Pacific Northwest for most of her life. She and her husband reside in a small town where she enjoys Bible reading and learning from God's Word. Her hobbies include flower gardening and landscaping, home improvement projects, baking desserts, and reading inspirational nonfiction and fiction. A favorite pastime is sitting on their home's deck to drink in the peace and beauty of nature. Her passion in writing is to use stories to help others see the mercy and goodness of God.

Lin Daniels retired after 39 years of teaching physical education, mostly at the elementary school level. For the past seven years, she has enjoyed writing, preaching on occasion, and working with the church youth group. An avid golfer, she and her twin sister, play several days a week. They especially delight in playing as partners and dress almost identically except for one small item (maybe a different color hat)! After all, you have to "zig and zag" a bit as teammates. Another of Lin's passions is pickle ball — a tennis-like game played on a smaller court with a whiffle ball.

Lola Di Giulio De Maci is a retired teacher whose stories have appeared in numerous editions of the *Chicken Soup for the Soul,* and *Divine Moments* series, *Guideposts, Reminisce, Los Angeles Times,* children's publications, and newspaper columns. Lola has a Master of Arts in Education and English, and a Doctorate in Education. She writes overlooking the San Bernardino Mountains.

Diana Derringer is an award-winning writer and author of *Beyond Bethlehem and Calvary: 12 Dramas for Christmas, Easter, and More!* Her articles, devotions, dramas, planning guides, Bible studies, and poems have been accepted more than 1,000 times by 70+ publications including *The Upper Room, The Secret Place, Clubhouse, Kentucky Monthly, Country, Missions Mosaic,* and several anthologies. She also writes radio drama for Christ to the World Ministries.

Her adventures as a social worker, adjunct professor, youth Sunday school teacher, and friendship family for international university students supply a constant flow of writing ideas. Visit her at dianaderringer.com. You can also find her on Facebook, Twitter, LinkedIn, Instagram, Goodreads, Pinterest, and her Amazon page.

Ellen Fannon is an award-winning author, retired veterinarian, former missionary, and church pianist/organist. She and her retired Air Force pilot-turned-pastor husband have fostered more than 40 children and have two adopted sons. Ellen has published eight novels, and her stories have appeared in *One Christian Voice, Chicken Soup for the Soul,* the *Divine Moments* series, and *Guideposts.* Her devotions have appeared in *Open Windows,* Guideposts' *God's Creatures,* and *The Secret Place.*

Visit Ellen's website, *Good for a Laugh*, and sign up to follow her weekly blog at ellenfannonauthor.com

Glenda Ferguson graduated from Chamois High School, College of the Ozarks, and Indiana University. Her mother was her greatest encourager in every dream Glenda pursued. Glenda's work has appeared in *All God's Creatures, Angels on Earth, Chicken Soup for the Soul, Sasee,* and the *Short and Sweet* and *Divine Moments* series. The Indiana Arts Commission has included her poem "The Buffalo Trace Trail: Then and Now" in the INverse Poetry Archive. Glenda receives virtual encouragement from the Writers Forum of Burton Kimble Farms Education Center. As a volunteer with Indiana Landmarks, she conducts tours of two historical hotels. She and her husband, Tim, live in southern Indiana.

Phil Gladden retired with his wife and eight cats and moved to Paris, Kentucky. He writes a weekly column for the *Bourbon County Citizen*. He writes his stories from his porch so people can make sense of small daily acts and facts that we overlook in pursuit of larger and perhaps even unattainable goals. By writing to transport others to a world that is both real and ideal, he shows how writing about a June bug may give more meaning to life than writing about superheroes, former presidents, and cataclysmic events. His book *Think About It*, a collection of articles, essays, and short stories, is available through Amazon.

Lydia E. Harris has been married to her college sweetheart, Milt, for more than 50 years. She enjoys spending time with her family, which includes two married children and five grandchildren. She is the author of three books for grandparents: *Preparing My Heart for Grandparenting: for Grandparents at Any Stage of the Journey, In the Kitchen with Grandma: Stirring Up Tasty Memories Together,* and *GRAND Moments: Devotions Inspired by Grandkids.*

With a master's degree in Home Economics, Lydia creates

and tests recipes with her grandchildren for Focus on the Family children's magazines. She also pens the column "A Cup of Tea with Lydia," which is published in the U.S. and Canada. It's no wonder she is known as "Grandma Tea."

Helen L. Hoover squeezes writing in between sewing, reading, knitting, and tending her flower and veggie gardens. She and Larry, her husband of 62 years, are retired and live in the Ozark Mountains of south-central Missouri. They enjoy visits with their two living children, and their grandchildren and great-grandchildren. Helen has had articles published in 18 books in the *Divine Moments* series, and devotionals and personal articles in *Word Aflame*, *The Secret Place*, *Word Action Publication*, *The Quiet Hour*, *The Lutheran Digest*, *Light and Life Communications*, *Chicken Soup for the Soul*, and *Victory in Grace*.

Penny L. Hunt is an accomplished writer whose award-winning, bestselling Amazon.com books, featured magazine articles, and contributions to numerous anthologies — including *Chicken Soup for the Soul* and *Guideposts* — reflect her passion for Christ and storytelling. Her work spans both children's and adult literature, resonating with a broad audience. Penny uses experiences from her years abroad, everyday moments, and the profound lessons they offer, to craft engaging and heartfelt narratives in the hope of enriching others' lives. A devoted follower of Christ, mother of five, and wife of a retired career naval officer/attaché, Penny enjoys cooking, gardening, and embracing life in the rural peach-growing region of South Carolina with her husband, Bill, and their two rescue dogs. Contact her at www.PennyLHunt.com.

Sherry Diane Kitts, originally from southwest Virginia near the Blue Ridge Mountains, currently resides with her husband in central Florida. Sherry writes non-fiction short stories and devotions, and has been published in several anthologies. She belongs to Word Weavers International, and the Ocala Chapter. She writes about navigating life's journey through seasons of labor, love, learning, and laughter. Sherry hopes others receive joy and encouragement as they read and relate to her experiences.

Bob LaForge became a Christian in 1977. He and his wife, Toni, have twin daughters, Sarah and Danielle, born in 2006. The family attends Grace Bible Church where Bob oversees the bookstore and teaches Adult Sunday School.

He has over 300 publications and has written three books which are available on Amazon.com: *Contemplating the Almighty* which discusses who and what God is, *Developing Great Relationships*, and the novel *The Tempter Comes*. Church Growth Institute published "Evaluating Your Friendship Skills."

Bob's books, articles, devotions, several Bible study series, a section on Bible literacy, and tracts are available for free download on his website:, www.disciplescorner.com.

Laura Lee Leathers, freelance writer, speaker, and writers' mentor, describes herself as Lois Lane over 65, and living on a farm. Her metropolis is the arena of freelance writing. Laura's primary love interest is the Word of God. She digs for information, interviews fascinating people, offers a cup of biblical hospitalit-tea, encourages, and helps others with the "how-to's" of life. Visit her website at: www.lauraleeleathers.com and sign up for the weekly newsletter.

Iris Long is a 65-year-old grandmother who lives in Memphis, Tennessee. She has a daughter, a son, and one grandson, age 10, who is a delight to the entire family. Iris worked as a medical transcriptionist for 37 years and has served as a caregiver for the past six years. She enjoys sharing God's love story with others.

Her first book, published in 2015, reveals how the grace of God prevented the anguish and mistakes of her past from destroying her future when He rescued her through His love and brought healing and transformation. Iris' second book, now being prepared for publication, chronicles her commitment to grow in Christlikeness, following a path only visible by faith.

Terry Magness can't hide the fact that she loves her family, people, and thoroughly enjoys writing, finding it not only cathartic, but also a wonderful means of discovery, awareness, and a great way of connecting people.

A contributor to the *Short and Sweet* and *Divine Moments* anthologies, Terry has authored two books: *Azadiah Reynolds — God's Jamaica Man,* and *Ever Increasing Grace.* She is a writer for the Assemblies of God, Southern Missouri Ministry Network's *Refresh Ministry Women* blog for credentialed women, missionaries, and pastors' wives, and leads one of their weekly online Refresh Connect groups.

Terry is founder of Grace Harbour Ministries, a biblically-based teaching, discipleship, and prayer ministry to women. An ordained minister, she serves in Biblical pastoral counseling, mentoring, coaching, and teaching.

Amannda Gail Maphies works at the UMKC School of Pharmacy, is a mother to two sons, and two pets — a dog, and a cat. She enjoys freelance writing based on her travels, life adventures, and pretty much anything that stands out in life as "story-worthy." Manndi contributes to several online and print publications, including: *Ozarks Farm and Neighbor, Connections Magazine, Raising Teens Today., Parenting Teens and Tweens, Moms of Teens and Tweens, Her View from Home, Salt + Sparrow, Focus on the Family, The Christian Standard,* among several others, and has been published in *Chicken Soup for the*

Soul's Believing in Angels. Her first book, *Tales from My Mummy*, was published in September 2022 and is available through local bookstores and on Amazon Kindle.

Norma C. Mezoe has been a published writer for 39 years. She became a Christian at the age of 15, but didn't grow spiritually in a significant way until a crisis, at the age of 33, brought her into a closer relationship with the Lord. Her desire is to honor God with her writing, and to encourage and point others to Jesus Christ. She writes regularly for *Christian Devotions.us*. Her work has also been published in several of the *Divine Moments* anthologies, devotionals, Sunday school take-home papers, magazines, and online. Norma may be contacted at: normacm@tds.net.

Majetta Morris began writing as a student for the high school newspaper. She developed and wrote curriculum for both school and church as she taught in school for over 25 years and served in Children's Ministries for over 50 years. Upon retirement, Majetta became the General Editor for SOMO Assemblies of God Women's *Refresh* blog, as well as a freelance editor who helps new writers to publish. Her students have won awards; her editorial clients have been published. Contact her at bright.light.editing.coach@gmail.com.

Vicki H. Moss is former Editor-at-Large and Contributing Editor for *Southern Writers Magazine* where she interviewed authors and contributed articles on writing in addition to blogging for the magazine's *Suite T* blog. She also wrote a weekly column as a pundit for the *American Daily Herald*. As a workshop instructor for writing conferences, Vicki teaches from her books *How to Write for Kids' Magazines* and *Writing with Voice*. With over 750 articles published, she co-authored the book *nailed It!* and contributed to Cecil Murphey's book, *I Believe in Heaven*. When Vicki's not making author visits or teaching a class on "Writing the Stories Behind the Recipes," gardening, and writing prose, she writes poetry that's published in magazines and her books on writing.

Peggy Park was born on a cotton farm in Mississippi, the fourth of five children. After nursing school and marriage she moved to Lexington, Kentucky when her husband joined the Lexington Clinic as a physician. Peggy was a full time mom until her last child was in junior high, at which time she returned to nursing. She spent nine years in part time bedside nursing at University of Kentucky Markey cancer center.

Peggy leads a Grief Share group at her church. Her husband, George died four years ago so she is well acquainted with the struggles in grieving.

Her writing includes a reflection posted every two weeks on her web site www.parkpraisepublications.com. She emails subscribers monthly and writes for her church paper.

Madonna Pool retired in 2018 from more than 46 years in nursing. She then began writing modernized reflections on some part of the Christmas story each year and reading them to her grandchildren on Christmas Eve.

Although retired, her schedule is filled with Bible studies, ministering activities in her Catholic parish, and committee work. She recently became a member of DAR (Daughters of the American Revolution), and plans to become more involved in this patriotic service organization.

Madonna lives in League City, Texas with her husband of almost 55 years. Their daughter's family — which includes their two grandchildren — also live in League City, and their son resides in Nashville, Tennessee.

Heather Roberts is a pediatric occupational therapist in the school system. Her work has been published by Focus on the

Family, *Guideposts, Christian Devotions, Prayer Connect, The Secret Place, Unlocked,* Grace Publishing, Cross River Media, and more.

Heather cherishes time spent in pursuing God. In addition to her writing, she works in the children's and prayer ministry at her church and leads several local and international prayer groups.

You can often find her scoping out people's landscaping and dreaming of adding another garden. She is the mother of four and wife to an amazing husband. Chocolate is her nemesis.

Check out her website, https://heathernroberts.com, where she writes about encouraging insights she receives from the Lord. She's also on Instagram at heather.n.roberts, and Facebook.

Beverly Robertson's high school English class first sparked her interest in writing when fellow students selected her essay "Teachers" to be published in the local paper. However, her stories smoldered in a file cabinet until after her retirement as an elementary school teacher's aide.

Then her writing ignited. She pulled out her stories on biblical women, put them together in an anthology, and self-published *Bible Brides: Trials and Triumphs.* For her church women's group, she presented a monthly lesson on different women of the Bible. Beverly's had a short story appear in *Whatever Lovely* magazine, and Christmas stories in the *Divine Moments'* books *Celebrating Christmas* and *Christmas Spirit.* She networks and hones her writing skills as a member of American Christian Fiction Writers.

Desiree St. Clair Spears has written for numerous publications including *Guideposts,* the *Short and Sweet* series, *A Joy-Full Season, The Times-Crescent* newspaper, and her church blog. A recently-retired high school career and technology education teacher, Desiree has more than 30 years of experience teaching all ages from infant to adult. She earned her M.A. at Notre Dame of Maryland University and her B.S. at Salisbury University.

Desiree is active in her church, serving as trustee, greeter, and leader of a women's small group. She recently celebrated her second anniversary with her husband, Robert, and is the mother of three adult children and grandmother of eleven. In addition to spoiling the grandkids, she enjoys traveling, walking, and life on the farm. Visit her blog at http://desireeglass.blogspot.com.

Gina Stinson is busy reclaiming every day for God's glory after years of living in fear and defeat. She is a pastor's wife of 31 years and mom of two young adults. Between family and ministry, she enjoys dabbling in gardening, crocheting, and playing music on her second-hand baby grand piano. As a storyteller for those who have overcome their circumstances and embraced God's goodness, she writes true stories of God's reclaiming power. Her first collection of storytelling devotions, *Reclaimed, The Stories of Rescued Moments and Days*, is available on Amazon. You can find her website at ginastinson.com; on Facebook at facebook.com/reclaimingeveryday, and on Instagram at instagram.com/reclaimingeveryday.

Annette G. Teepe is a writer, scientist, educator, hiker, and life-long learner. Her passion is teaching others through her writing and speaking skills. She hopes to inspire future generations of scientists by publishing science-topic books for elementary and middle school students. Annette is a member of the Bartlett (Tennessee) Christian Writers group and the National Association for Science Writers.

Kathy Tharpe and her husband moved 18 times as a military and government family, meeting a lot of interesting people along the way.

Kathy taught topical Bible study classes coordinating with lectures for the Christian Women of Berlin, an English-speaking nondenominational organization in Germany, and then later as the Teaching Leader for Community Bible Study International, when offered in Berlin as a bi-lingual program. Despite many differences, she found all women have a hunger for the Word.

After 11 years in Europe she is glad to be back in the U.S. and close to her extended family. She enjoys discovering new international dishes and making keepsake quilts for her college-bound grandchildren to take a little bit of home with them, no matter where they go.

Lauri Lemke Thompson, a Wisconsin native, appreciates living with her husband in the lovely Ozark mountains in Branson, Missouri. She is active in Christian Women's Connection (Stonecroft) and the Ozarks Chapter of the American Christian Writers. Her two books, *Hitting Pause* and *Pressing Forward*, are collections of her columns, articles and devotions. Her bimonthly column appears in the *Branson Globe* newspaper.

Nanette Thorsen-Snipes is a freelance editor, proofreader, and writer in the Christian publishing industry. She has contributed stories and devotions to more than 70 compilation books — Guideposts *Miracle* series, *Chicken Soup for the Soul*, *New Women's Devotional Bible*, among others — and has written dozens of magazine articles, devotions, and children's stories. Her stories have been in seven of the books in the *Divine Moments* series.

Donna Collins Tinsley, wife, mother and grandmother (with one great-grand) lives in Port Orange, Florida and has been included in magazines and book compilations, as well as on WAPN, 91.5 radio programs. Being a mother with children who love animals, she has re-named the backyard, The Pet Cemetery, because rabbits, dogs, cats, turtles and more are buried there. She is a member of Word Weavers International, Volusia County

Group. You can find her on Facebook, at Somebody's Mother Online Prayer Support Group, or her blog: *A Sister, A Mother, A Daughter Among You* (donnacollinstinsley.blogspot.com). Email her at Thornrose7@aol.com

Charlene Warren's career included experience in Social Services (MO) for 21 years. She and her husband of 60 years have four grown children and six grandchildren.

Over the years, Charlene taught primary-age girls in Sunday School and served as Coach in Hospitality Ministry. She currently leads a Ladies Life Group at her church.

Spiritual inspirations with the Lord led her to write poetry. Not a choice she would have chosen. She went on to publish a book titled *Treasures in My Garden*. Gospel Publishing has used several of her devotionals in their Adult Ministry. Focus on the Family published "Families in Ministry."

Her latest venture is a children's short story titled "Harry Caterpillar's Adventures."

If you enjoyed

A Gift of Love

you might also enjoy these
books in the *Divine Moments* Series

Divine Moments
Christmas Moments
Spoken Moments
Precious, Precocious Moments
More Christmas Moments
Stupid Moments
Additional Christmas Moments
Why? Titanic Moments
Loving Moments
Merry Christmas Moments
Cool-inary Moments
Moments with Billy Graham
Personal Titanic Moments
Remembering Christmas
Romantic Moments
Pandemic Moments
Christmas Stories
Broken Moments
Celebrating Christmas
Grandma's Cookie Jar
Can, Sir!
Christmas Spirit
Joy to the World
Lost . . . and Found
Treasured Moments

www.ingramcontent.com/pod-product-compliance
Lightning Source LLC
LaVergne TN
LVHW051604070426
835507LV00021B/2765